READ THIS!

Edited by Karen Zoppa

With a Preface by
John Ralston Saul

READ THIS!
Why Books Matter

J. GORDON SHILLINGFORD
PUBLISHING INC

Design and typography by Gallant Design Ltd.
Printed and bound in Canada.

We acknowledge the financial assistance of the Manitoba Arts Council and The Canada Council for the Arts for our publishing program.

CANADIAN CATALOGUING IN PUBLICATION DATA

Read this! : Why books matter / edited by Karen Zoppa.

ISBN 0-920486-53-3

1. English literature—Study and teaching—Canada. 2. English language—Study and teaching—Canada. 3. Reading—Canada. 4. Children—Books and reading—Canada. I. Zoppa, Karen Elizabeth, 1956-

PR35.R39 2003   820'.71'071   C2003-903953-6

J. Gordon Shillingford Publishing
P.O. Box 86, RPO Corydon Avenue, Winnipeg, MB Canada R3M 3S3

For the Readers and the Writers:

"So long as men can breathe and eyes can see,
So long lives this, and this gives life to thee."
-William Shakespeare

TABLE OF CONTENTS

IN DEFENCE OF
PUBLIC EDUCATION

His Excellency John Ralston Saul

W hat is the tragedy of a class-based society? Quite simply, it is a society which has institutionalized selfishness. We all have selfishness within us. We all have our self-interest. And we need it. But that is quite different from acting as if selfishness were the leitmotif of civilization. A healthy democracy is one which works to avoid that tragedy.

As for public education, it is a simile for civilized democracy. You could say that public education is the primary foundation in any civilized democracy. That was one of the great discoveries of western civilization in its modern form in the middle of the 19th century.

Any weakening of universal public education can only be a weakening of democracy.

I personally do not believe that citizens—Canadian citizens in particular—have any desire to abandon the true strengths of their society. I believe that there is a profound understanding in our society of the long-standing essential role universal public education plays in making us a civilized democracy.

Citizens live complex lives and have little free time. Yet they are obliged to deal with all of those fashions and ideologies which come along, grab hold of the mechanisms of public influence, and then set about undermining the fundamentals of civilization.

The ideologies of our day are comfortably ensconced in various schools of economics which have embraced late 19th century simplistic theories of inevitability. You can also find them in various schools of managerialism, which also are attached to a belief in the inevitability of events.

1

Floating around these economists and managers is a whole new class of what used to be called courtiers and are now called consultants. Some of them are operating out of what are called independent think tanks, financed in such a way that they are independent on behalf of those who finance them.

All of this represents a tidal wave of specialists who have drawn as their principal conclusion that inclusive systems which serve the public good are no longer viable. In other words, the ideologies and fashions of our day are devoted in good part to a return of the tragedy of the class-based society. They are devoted to weakening the universality of the very public education system which has made Canada such a remarkably successful society.

Let me point out something which is difficult to accept for many people who are themselves devoted to managing—and managing well—classes, schools and the school system. Managerialism encourages and rewards agreement among professionals. It admires discretion and conformity, it encourages us all to believe that through detailed work, we can rectify enormous problems.

Let me give you two examples of the contradictions this creates. We all agree on the need for small classrooms, particularly in this era of high immigration, ever more complex societies and ever more open borders. We need intense, personalized education. This seems to mean classes of twenty or less students.

Yet the managerial solutions of today are carrying us towards larger classrooms. Why? Because no matter how modern these managerial theories sound, they are usually rooted in the industrial theories of the late 19th century. And those theories are based upon a belief in economies of scale. What is more, we are consistently bombarded by statistics which assert that class sizes are not actually too big. This is where the business of discretion and conformity and attempting to solve problems behind the scene comes in. In most cases, those statistics are a form of gerrymandering.

The statisticians take the total number of accredited teachers and administrators, and divide them into the total number of students. But many of those included in the calculation never go into a classroom because they are principals, vice-principals, counsellors and so on. And so the official statistics talk of 25 or 30 students per class, when parents—that is citizens—know that their children are in classes of thirty five.

Let me give you another example of what happens when we buy into the closed arguments of inevitability. In school after school around the country it seems that there is ever less money for what are now described as the soft edges of education. Many of these soft edges were included automatically in education until a few years ago. Schools find themselves short of books and of equipment. They find that certain advanced classes are suddenly too expensive. Certain special needs are too special. Many extracurricular activities suddenly are beyond their budgets.

Principals, teachers and parents find themselves obliged to go out and raise money—i.e., engage in private fundraising. This presents two very real problems. The first is that raising funds for a public school in a middle or upper middle class neighbourhood is not all that difficult. Raising funds in a working class or lower middle class neighbourhood—or indeed a neighbourhood with many new immigrants trying very hard to begin their lives in Canada—is a much more difficult undertaking. The whole idea of private fundraising for public schools is the first step towards introducing a class based society into Canada. Private fundraising is, in and of itself, a form of exclusion.

Let me add a tougher comment. By going out and spending a great deal of their valuable time fundraising, principals, teachers and parents are actually collaborating in the gradual privatization of the public school system. They are making privatization easier for those who do not wish to take public responsibility for raising the necessary amounts of public money. I often feel we would do better to stand back and to say openly that this is a public system and that if society and its leaders are not willing to fund the system, then we collectively, and they specifically, must all take responsibility for the decline in the education of our own children and the children of our fellow citizens. Perhaps there is a need for citizens to stand back and say to the public authorities: It is your obligation to raise the funds and to deliver universal public education. It is not our responsibility to undermine that universality. Over to you.

Our country has been built, from the very beginnings of its democratic system 150 years ago, upon a happy linkage between democracy and public education. These are the basic principles of the Canadian democracy.

In the 19th century, we were a naturally poor country, working under the extremely difficult circumstances of our climate and geography. We constructed our prosperity consciously and intellectually. We constructed our success and we did so to a great extent through our public education system. Any move towards weakening that system will risk undermining not simply our society, but also our prosperity.

Our success as a country is built upon this system. It is only with great difficulty that I could imagine a greater betrayal of the principle of Canadian democracy than the piecemeal reduction of public education to private education.

There is one point on which there should be no misunderstanding. The concept of universality does not mean that everything must be the same. The strength of a public education system such as ours is that, being so large and serving so many different communities, it is capable of enormous diversities. We only have to look at the remarkable success story of French immersion over the last quarter century to see what our public system is capable of. Starting at zero, we have today over 320,000 students in French immersion.

Let me add to that the other large requirement of diversity in our society. This country has been built on a combination of its Aboriginal peoples and its immigrants. Most of those immigrants have come as reasonably poor people, very often illiterate or not speaking either of our official languages. The Saul's, for example, came here in the middle of the 19th century as virtually illiterate stone masons. My family, like yours I'm sure, is a product of the public school system.

We citizens take the responsibility of inviting people from around the world to come to join us in Canada. We're the host. The primary obligation and responsibility is ours, as it is with any host. We offer these newcomers an open, inclusive society in which the citizens can act as citizens, can speak out, become involved in public life as they wish, and perhaps do well economically. We have three primary obligations when we invite immigrants to come to join us here. First, to ensure that our democratic system and its values are clearly understandable and accessible to them. Second, to ensure that our public systems work. Third, to provide an intense, inclusive public education system which will allow them and their children to adjust to Canadian society. All the state has to provide are public systems which work and a good education system. The immigrant or citizen does all the rest. My family, like yours, is the proof that this is a bargain which no self-respecting democracy can turn its back on.

One of the particularities of Canada is that we have many levels of government, as befits the second largest landmass in the world with a reasonably small population, two official languages and three founding peoples. The system is as it should be. And fundamentally it works well. After all, we are the second or third oldest democracy in the world.

One of the specific realities of this system is that the responsibility for education was given, from the beginning, to the provinces and territories. This ensures that the regional nature of Canada is not overwhelmed, as it was in most parts of Europe, by monolithic, centralizing theories of state and mythology. Our civilization is intended to be complicated and the regionalization of our education system allows it to maintain that complexity.

What this means is that the primary arm for the creation of citizens, whether children of people born in Canada or immigrants, lies in the hands of the provinces. It is their most important responsibility. And it is regional, national and international at the same time.

You may be for or against globalization. But at the end of the day, the ability of our young citizens to face the various effects of the opening of borders lies in the hands of the provincial and territorial governments. That is, it lies in their obligation to provide universal public education; to maintain the century and a half-old tradition of a middle class egalitarian inclusive society. And it means that we have to provide a very complex education: we need to produce kids who can read a minimum of two languages, probably English and French, but they probably should have three or four to go anywhere or to do anything internationally. They have to have in-depth education in thought, philosophy, history, the social-political economics of Asia and northern Europe, *literature*—a very complex education. Otherwise, they can't go out into a win-win situation.

Today we have a largely urban population. Our cities are filled with a highly mobile population, two job families, high divorce levels, single parent families, the return of long hours of work, the loss of community identification, high immigration levels, a new rise in the division between rich and poor and so on. All of these factors mean that the one—if not the only—public structure we have which is capable of reaching out to all citizens in all parts of the country and making them feel part of the extended family of citizenship is the public education system. In the classic sense of the inclusive democracy, those simple brick and mortar buildings, which we call the public schools, are in fact the one remaining open club house of citizenship. Not only is the public education system and its fundamental structure not old fashioned, it has found a new form of modernity. I would argue that we are more reliant on it today than we were through most of the 20th century.

We must turn away from the mediocre and tired management theories of efficiency through economies of scale. We must particularly be wary of their latest manifestation which preaches training rather than education. If you spend a lot of time training kids on machines, you know perfectly well that by the time they get out of school, the machines are going to be obsolete. In the meantime, they haven't learned how to dance on one foot and think of six things at once, which is what they'll need to do in an unstable, changing world economy, where they're going to have to move their career five or six times in different directions. Philosophy and literature are far more useful than turning a machine on and off.

We need more than ever to look at the public education system as the primary tool we have to ensure that children are able to grow up to become citizens.

INTRODUCTION

"I am having such a hard time getting my child to read at home," she said, a tinge of urgency in her voice. "Maybe it's the video games, or the 3000 channel universe, but I can't seem to entice him into spending time with a book. When he was in primary school, we would curl up together with his book bag and it was such fun! But now that he is in Grade 7, he doesn't want to talk to me, and the books are no longer coming home. What can I do?"

What indeed can she, or any of us, do? Why aren't the books coming home anymore? In the primary grade English curriculum, books remain the vital instrument of language development. But in the middle and senior years programmes, books—those repositories of excellent prose, sustained narrative, imaginative journeys and clear argument—are increasingly being sidelined in favour of the one-page magazine article, the advertisement, the video and the graph. The present English language arts curriculum has added two new "language arts" to the previous list of listening, speaking, reading and writing: now, students will "view and represent." But how does one "view and represent" or read and write in a

> "Language is the primary instrument of thought and the primary basis in all communication...: ("Manitoba Curriculum Framework of Outcomes and Senior 4 Standards," 4).

way that engages confident use of the English language, if one is never exposed to the most salient forms of it that we find in books?

This parent is a reader herself who models reading in the home, and expects her children to become lifelong readers. Consider how this situation is compounded for the child who does not come from a reading family, and who is exposed to the same onslaught of electronic and other imagery this parent laments. Consider how many high school students, at the time that books start to become more peripheral in the upper grades, experience a decline in mastery of basic conventions of spelling, syntax and usage. Consider that the high schools students of today will become the teachers of tomorrow.

What can we do?

In 1997, an inspired Deborah Schnitzer, University of Winnipeg Professor of English, called a meeting of first year university English teachers and secondary English teachers to establish an on-going forum for communicating our shared aspirations, difficulties and practices in the English classroom. Thus MACRO—the Meaningful Assessment and Curricular Reform Organization—was born. In the course of our early discussions, we grew to see that we all belonged to the same educational continuum, and that we were all experiencing a common frustration with the level of literacy our 17, 18 and 19 year old students possessed. Our common diagnosis was that our students were no less intelligent, creative and critically aware than previously, but because they live in a situation of unprecedented exposure to electronic media, they consequently seem to read less. We observed that not only do many of them seem to read less, but they are reading less literature—fewer full-length fiction and non-fiction works. More alarming, they are reading fewer and fewer books in school.

It was around the same time that Manitoba Education and Training began piloting the new "outcomes" based curriculum and the standards exams so eminently suited to assessing such outcomes. MACRO analyzed and evaluated these exams, concluding that they amounted to a very expensive and counter-productive way to assess reading comprehension and writing proficiency, an assessment undertaken much more comprehensively and continually by classroom teachers anyway. We

> "At all grades, the focus has shifted from reading, writing, and the study of literature to an emphasis on acquiring language and literary skills through listening, speaking, viewing, and representing, as well as reading and writing" (1).

lobbied the government to acknowledge how deficient these tests are and how they misdirect classroom energy away from more vital, sustained and demanding language arts education.

We were not alone. Parents and educators, including members of the Manitoba Teachers Society, articulated parallel concerns. In large measure, our joint representations of those concerns led to the cancellation of mandatory standards tests in grades 3, 6 and 9 in this province, an effort that demonstrates our commitment to authentic assessment. We also saw that there is an obvious link between standards tests and the "outcomes" based curriculum, and an even deeper link between this instrumental version of education and a willingness to impose an industrial model on all of our social enterprises.

In this view of education and society, reading and writing are merely instrumental. We want Johnny to be able to write the manual, or read the executive summary, but we certainly don't want to waste his time with fluff, like novels or reflective nonfiction, which may cause him to question his assumptions or fritter away his time through a vicarious adventure. Even if we do allow for the entertainment value of literature, we want to focus on those things that can be measured, and a grasp of irony, a feeling for poetic rhythm, a love of syntactic clarity, not to mention ideas, are not easily measured. Unlike the 56 Outcomes.

The English Language Arts Framework of Curriculum Outcomes cites 56 specific outcomes, grouped under five broad headings, that students are "mandated" to achieve. The individual "outcomes" are for the most part labels given to discrete skills involved in language facility—punctuation, parallelism, subject-verb agreement, audience, voice, tone and so on. As experienced teachers know, most of these "outcomes" are not "achieved" in isolation but are acquired organically, seamlessly, through exposure to, and the practice of, listening, speaking, reading and writing. One might think, where is the problem? Students will read and write and talk and listen anyway, and they will acquire mastery of these outcomes along the way, which we can then "measure" individually through the standards tests. The assumption here is that such "skills" can be engaged without any meaningful reference to content. Ironically, this focus on decoding skills at the expense of the content such skills are meant to serve has contributed to the erasure of written texts, particularly books, in some classrooms.

The present curriculum's implicit devaluing of literature is in part due to its muddy and deficient theory of discourse, one fraught with internal ambiguity and contradiction. The previous curriculum fairly represented the clear, flexible and accessible rhetorical model proposed by scholars such as James Kinneavey. According to this model, all discourse aims to express, persuade or inform. Depending on the purpose of the communication, one will emphasize the expressive need of the author, the context of the audience or the content demands of the subject. Because we often have overlapping intentions in communicating, one can, for example, write a poem that expresses and persuades, or an essay that informs while expressing a personal sensibility and style. The important thing is to be mindful of what your primary purpose is, and to construct your communication accordingly. All written and spoken genres can be placed within any of the three basic aims of communication. In this model, then, a novel can simultaneously act as a source of information, an act of persuasion and a personal expression.

Contrast this with the "theory" given in the present curriculum. According to this document, the three "language uses" are the expressive, which "is not used primarily to communicate," the transactional/ pragmatic, "the language of getting things done" and the aesthetic, "expressive language shaped and crafted to capture and represent experiences." (4) Leaving aside the absurdity of identifying a *language use* which is not used to communicate, the remaining two categories are presented as a dichotomy, where "pragmatic" uses are transparent, obvious and desirable, while "aesthetic" uses are opaque, obtuse and optional. In this model, all "texts" are either "pragmatic" or "aesthetic," and it is clear most books, whether fiction or not, will fall into the latter, less desirable, category.

The curriculum further erodes the role of books by defining "text" in a manner so broad that one can call a billboard a "text" today and be perfectly justified in claiming that your students are "reading" a "text." It is not unreasonable to recognize that any phenomenon that requires decoding is on some level a "text." However, in the English language arts classroom, it is also not unreasonable to assume that the English language will be the chief focus of attention, and that the reading of excellent written language is an irreplaceable activity in the development of students' language proficiency, not to mention their humanity.

This broad definition of "text" is a corollary of the impossible expectations placed on the English language arts classroom today. English teachers are expected to address media literacy, film literacy, and visual art literacy as well as all of the more conventional language processes in the course of the year. Is it any wonder that so many of our students read so little when the curriculum itself discourages them from doing so?

Finally, this curriculum and the standards exams which measure it imply that content in the English classroom is irrelevant. It doesn't matter what they read, so long as they dot their "i"s at the end of the day. And yet why would one care about dotting the "i" unless it serves something important that is being said? What about the other gifts literature brings to the human being who is also the student: the broadening of the sympathies, the expansion of the imagination, the community of shared literary experience?

Over a period of three years, MACRO lobbied successive Ministers of Education to listen to and act on our concern about the eroded place of books in the curriculum. At the time of this writing, Manitoba Education and Training has recently revised the Senior 4 Framework document to stipulate those occasions when books are the preferred "text." This is a needed correction to a curriculum whose ambiguity on the centrality of books in the English classroom allowed some teachers to leave them out altogether. However, this revision does not address the more serious deficiencies of the curriculum, nor does it acknowledge that perhaps the most important lessons are of things that cannot be measured. The present curriculum still does not acknowledge that standards tests based on 56 outcomes engage too little of the learning that takes place when specific books are read in specific classroom communities with specific, concrete, authentic guidelines and assessment activities in place to explore their implications.

These issues are presented from within the context of Manitoba. However, the movement towards outcomes and standards tests, and the consequences in English classrooms, is a global phenomenon among English speaking countries. In Canada, Manitoba Education and Training is the lead writing team for the Western Protocol—the curricula subscribed to by all four western provinces. In Ontario and some eastern provinces, the situation is much the same.

Given these critical issues, MACRO will continue to work towards developing a curriculum that encourages reading and all the gifts of literacy this brings, a curriculum that will guide in the best way the innate abilities of our students, our future citizens in this splendid, flawed and glorious democracy. In the meantime, we offer you the opportunity to "read this" volume of reflections on the power of books in our schools and lives. And if the spirit moves you, we encourage you to join us in re-visioning our schools.

Karen Zoppa, Executive Editor
with Valdine Clemens, Dee Gillies, Shawn Kettner, Catherine Froese-Klassen,
Deborah Schnitzer, and Phyllis Webster
Autumn 2003

"…language, called "expressive language," is used not primarily to communicate, but to make all meaning of experience and to construct a coherent and predictable view of the world" (4).

TEACHING NOVELS IN THE CLASSROOM: OUR CURRENT FICTIONS ABOUT THE READING PUBLIC

Neil Besner

Despite George Orwell's having reversed the last two digits in order to give *1984* its title, I thought it might be an interesting tactic in the fall term of that year to teach the novel, along with several other well-known dystopian novels, in a half-course introduction to fiction at Mount Royal College in Calgary. I remember two of the other novels: Arthur Koestler's grim meditation on Stalinist Russia, *Darkness at Noon*, and Anthony Burgess's *A Clockwork Orange*. I'm ashamed now to remember that the course was a big success. In its aftermath, I was invited to a local high school class to talk about *1984*, and that same fall at the College, we put on "An Evening in *1984*," a discussion of the novel by a political scientist, a prominent local journalist, the President of the College and myself. As these kinds of events go, it was also a big success, attracting an audience of maybe two hundred, and it was broadcast live on an educational channel (and rerun so many times that year that it began to turn into a parody of itself). Thinking about the event nearly twenty years later, I regret what now seems a gimmick course with its pretentious theme (and I regret "An Evening in *1984*" for related reasons), because to my mind they signalled the onset of a loss of faith in the real and more various powers of fiction to stand on their own; worse, they might have signalled a loss of belief in a teacher's ability to reveal these powers, or in his readers' abilities to discern them. And I wonder now whether a related series of disbeliefs—more recent, more general, and more insidious descendants of those earlier ones—underwrites our current and apparently growing unwillingness to teach novels in high school.

Set aside for a moment the tepid arguments, passionately pronounced by earnest educators across the land, about the dire influences of television and the web, and the consequent and equally dire pronouncements on children's drastically waning spans of attention. (The popularity of the Harry Potter novels, for starters, might give pause to these glib polemicists.) Set aside the equally earnest assertion (if misguided assumption) that teachers simply do not have the time to teach a whole novel in grades ten, eleven, or twelve, because they need this time to teach most students the more useful reading and writing skills they will need very soon: the job application, the resume, the memorandum, the executive summary. Set aside, as well, the devout but arid insistence on competitive standards, testing for standards, and the hellish road to "excellence" paved by these measures. None of these arguments should mitigate the place of the book, and of teaching books, in the language and literature classroom. (But they do.)

I think that in the current climate, there are more longstanding perceptions of booklength fictions at work. What idea of the book—for my purposes, what idea of the most popular contemporary literary form, the novel—might be animating our current debates about its place in the classroom? And why else, aside from the thin but immediate allure of the arguments outlined above, might the teaching of novels be falling into disfavour?

I'd like to advance several more fundamental (and, in the very worst sense of the term, fundamentalist) possibilities for our current attitudes towards the teaching of books of fiction. The first is what I understand as the considerable, and growing contemporary power of instrumentalist conceptions of the roles of reading and writing—in fact, of language. In the jargon of contemporary curricula, the "mastery" of "language skills" —I quote the terms because they are well worth examining for their implications, but that is a subject for another day—is too often thought to be the most important goal of the "English" classroom. It was the Mexican philosopher Santayana who defined the fanatic as he who, having lost sight of the ends, redoubles the means; it often seems to me that the instrumentalist curriculum of the high school English classroom emerges from just such an exclusive, if not near-fanatical, focus on the pragmatic, useful, applied understanding of language.

> "Text refers to all language forms that can be experienced, discussed and analyzed. These include print texts, oral texts such as storytelling, dialogues, speeches, and conversations, and visual texts such as pictures, diagrams, tableaux, mime and non-verbal communication"(7).

The second possibility, I think, has deeper historical roots both in North American culture generally and particularly in Canadian culture, and it is a longstanding distrust, misapprehension, at times an outright fear, of works of imagination, particularly verbal ones, and most particularly, of the place, power and function of stories. It was Catharine Parr Traill, the doughty and no-nonsense sister of the more melancholy Susanna Moodie, who advised, in the 1836 collection of letters known as *The Backwoods of Canada*, that Canada was no place for works of imagination because, essentially, it was very cold, it had no history or culture, and people had too much practical work at hand to waste their time with idle, leisure-class pursuits like reading and writing stories.

The Strickland sisters, interestingly, recur over and over again in modern Canadian writing. Catharine, or "C.P.T." appears as an admonitory, no-nonsense apparition in Margaret Laurence's 1974 novel *The Diviners*, sternly advising the protagonist-writer Morag Gunn to be up and doing rather than brood over her life. Her sister Susanna, author of the fascinating 1852 hybrid, *Roughing It in the Bush*, appears as the central speaker and character in Atwood's fine 1970 book of poems, *The Journals of Susanna Moodie*. She is also the subject of novelist Carol Shields's first book of criticism in 1976, *Susanna Moodie: Voice and Vision*. Here, to begin with, are several books well worth reading and studying in high school; but I digress.

This perennial distrust of works of the imagination arises and recedes in our culture in rhythms that have much to do with wider as well as more local economic and political developments. This distrust is particularly, I would argue, of verbal works of imagination such as the novel, because novels so often unsettle and interrogate theories and models of language that are merely transactional, applied or purely referential. Not insignificantly, two of the dystopian novels I alluded to above—*A Clockwork Orange* and *1984*—embed either a critique of language, the invention of an idiom or an inquiry into semantics as a powerful element in their dissections of their respective cultures. When the culture feels itself threatened from without, as it does now and as it will for the foreseeable future, one predictable but dangerous response is to batten down the hatches. It will insist on one (standard) meaning for each word and one word for each (homogenized) meaning. It will understand ambiguity and plurality as subversive of plainspeaking and it will relegate storymaking, reading, writing and thinking about stories to the realm of frivolity or genteel time-wasting that Catharine Parr Traill identified and lamented a 165 years ago. Distrust of the imagination is not new; nor is an insistence on standards and testing in education. But their unhappy confluence, the latter explicit and the former implied in that explicitness, can be fatal to the perception of fiction—and the teaching of fiction—as a fundamental component of many courses in literature at every level, from middle school through graduate school and beyond.

But set aside this kind of vapid theorizing, too. And set aside Catharine Parr Traill's warnings against indulging in flights of fancy in an allegedly no-nonsense place like our own. I would advocate strongly for the teaching of books, particularly of novels of all kinds, for a myriad of other reasons. The first among these, with Roland Barthes, is the sheer and unique pleasure of the text: the rich and many-minded pleasures of reading. There is simply no other way into the mind, being, body, soul, spirit or psyche of other human beings—no way that involves, not only language, but all of our senses, apprehensions and intuitions—that allows us as many avenues, alleyways and broad boulevards (and, yes, dead end streets) into meaning as the form of story we call the novel. There is no other kind of book—and there are many other kinds of book that I consider nearly as urgent if not indispensable to an education today (the biography, the autobiography, the history, the religious text)—that conveys its reader along the essential arc of a story, a life's story, more than a novel. There is no other form that at once teaches; exhilarates; damns; exalts; informs; arbitrates and discriminates;

inquires, critiques, interrogates, philosophizes, moralizes and more. There is no more profound exploration of the powers and possibilities for relationships and love, and of what prevents and forestalls love. There is no other kind of book that is so manyminded, multifarious—that can at once educate, instruct and delight (and chastise, condemn, damn). In the pantheon of contemporary art forms, the novel (and its visual first cousin, the film), comes closest to conveying and inquiring into, constituting and analyzing, a whole world. The good novel (and there is a plethora of good novels in the world, past and present) is the best and most constant corrective I know to the dark and growing convictions that language is just words; stories are just made up; memory is always false; and history is dead.

To read a good novel—to read it and discuss it in the company of others like and unlike yourself—is to enter the always unfinished conversation with your culture that you are participating in at this moment, willing or not. In the last two weeks, while travelling in South America, I read two recent novels by Canadians and a story by a classic Brazilian writer: Manitoban novelist David Bergen's *The Case of Lena S.*, Dennis Bock's *The Ash Garden* and a wonderful "tale" by Machado de Assis. As I write, these fictions are at work with me, doing what good fiction does: it reads you. Bergen's novel (set in Winnipeg) is quietly, powerfully and relentlessly pushing me to understand what happened to Lena—which means trying to understand Lena, her family, her sometime lover, Mason, and several others; and alongside these inquiries, the novel, like any good novel, is pushing me to read and reread myself. Meanwhile, I am trying to understand what I did not like about *The Ash Garden*, and in the process, I am, inescapably and inevitably, thinking again about Hiroshima, the bomb, and war, which is forcing me to think about contemporary Iraq. And to think about how to think; about how and why we tell, and read, and need stories; and about how we teach, and are taught stories, too.

One vital way in which we read, teach, tell and talk about stories is in the classroom. I think—I know—that we become fuller human beings by engaging in this activity. And I know that to reduce, limit or banish our access to novels in the classroom is perverse—for all of us. Reading is really a lot like breathing, and we're not at our best when we're short of breath. If life is very much like a story in the arc it traces between cradle and grave, then the novel is the contemporary form best suited to show us the shape of that arc. Teach novels to people you wish to live real lives. And if you don't want to teach novels, please go and teach in another area; don't justify your anemia by hiding behind so-called progressive curricular reform. Novels—like the people who write them, read them and talk about them—are too rare and vital a resource to entrust to the blind judgement of zealous time-management teams, standard bearers or platoons of egregious examiners. Without gimmick or apology, novels belong in classrooms as surely as do students and teachers. Let us keep them all there. It will make for a better and more literate world—for all of us.

READ THIS!

DEAR STUDENTS

Marg Rose

January 15, 2003

Dear Lucky Students:

I am writing to remind you of the luxury you are being offered, a free gift from the rest of us who are working each day in the offices and workplaces around you.

You are being given the chance to use part of your day to READ a BOOK. Many of the people I work with see this as an impossible dream. I work to help thousands of adults who would sacrifice mightily to be in your shoes.

As some of the 107,000 Manitobans who did not have the opportunity to start high school, these men and women often talk dreamily about how they would love to be able to read a whole book. They see books as a magical tool that will help them escape through their imaginations, or to be able to help their children with their homework, or to understand this culture more fully, or as part of their course credentials to prepare for further training. To them, books are the key that opens doors to a better future. In fact, one of Winnipeg's most successful free literacy programs is called Open Doors, just for that reason.

Another quarter of a million adults in Manitoba did not get the chance to finish their Grade 12 diploma. Over the past three years, about 15,000 adults have signed up to try to complete high school once again, by enrolling in dozens of adult learning centres. But now they have more barriers that get in the way of reaching their goals.

They often have to travel outside their neighborhoods, so transportation costs and timing becomes more difficult. Almost half of them have problems arranging and financing child care. Their lives are much more complicated. "I was working a lot of hours and was exhausted when I came home from work. Then I'd have to take care of things at home. I have two little kids. I couldn't really afford babysitting. Maybe if they could provide child care," a 45 year old woman with less than her grade 4 education said.[1] Other barriers such as a lack of support, low self esteem, lack of program supports for disabilities, program waiting lists, the part-time nature of adult learning and underfunding—all these factors get in the way.

The International Adult Literacy Survey[2] showed that up to one in four Manitobans would not be able to finish a novel, even if they tried. These folks do not have the reading skills to be able to read about the glorious romance in *The Republic of Love*, written and set in Winnipeg by Carol Shields. Margaret Atwood's *The Edible Woman* remains out of reach, until some financeer creates a movie version. None will learn through someone else's struggle with the elements the hard lessons shown in *Banner in the Sky*—a book I still recall from my high school required reading list. Books, more than magazines or e-zines, offer the reader a chance to bond with a character, follow a full plot development, see growth and change and learn from others' struggles. They can be comforting, challenging and inspiring. They can change lives. "Yet it is by touching the imagination of the child that a good book can penetrate and light up the soul to make the difference, as Emily Dickenson once wrote, 'where the meanings are,'" Senator Landon Pearson enthused when speaking to an international forum on literature last year.[3]

One of Canada's leading thinkers gets even more passionate about the way that reading should be taught. Full books are the best solution, John Ralston Saul stated:

> We have to have more and more concentration on reading. There should be less and less studying of chapters extracted from novels, which is probably the saddest way to teach literature. More and more we must accept that the kids are really smart and that they can read whole novels really young,

before they know the subjunctive… It is through reading novels that it becomes possible to learn the role of grammar. We read first, then we learn specifics after.[4]

So, lucky students, enjoy this wonderful gift that your teachers and the taxpayers are offering you. Put up your feet and read. Close your eyes and dream. Savour this luxury. It is one that no one can ever take away from you, once you master this life-affirming technique of travelling through time and in other bodies. Be a master of your own destiny.

For help, or to help others, look under LEARN in your Yellow Pages and call, when you are ready to give the gift of reading to others in your community. Sharing this gift doubles the pleasure, I assure you.

Sincerely,
Marg Rose, Executive Director
Literacy Partners of Manitoba

"IS THERE A MOVIE?"

David Bergen

Every year I start off my Grade 12 literary class with "The End of Firpo in the World," a short story by George Saunders. In two pages, with perfect pitch, Saunders opens up the world of a twelve-year-old loser freak fatty who, in seeking his glory, is hit by a car and dies. Good solid fun. Many of the students like the story: "It's vulgar and sad and funny and short." By short they mean not too much description. It is as if movies and television have knocked out any tolerance for prolonged exposition. Short and snappy, that's what they want. Few of these kids will dive into Dostoevsky or Henry James.

When we study *1984* I get this: "The book is crap, it made me want to use it as a table prop"; "Way too descriptive, boring"; "Whoaa, this sucks big time"; "Hated it, boring and slow, all that description stuff, that stuff from The Book."

"It's a seminal book of the twentieth century," I cry out, and I read them the section where Winston meets Julia, the dark-haired girl, and then the piece where Winston is broken. Five out of thirty-three students end up liking the book. Not bad.

I want my students to love books. I throw titles and authors at them, hoping that something might stick. Sometimes it works. Marissa, one of the girls in my early morning class, is gaga over Sylvia Plath. For Christmas she got the Modern Library edition of *The Bell Jar* and since then she has carried the book around like a Bible. She proselytizes, tells others that they have to read it. "It's *amazing*," she says. She can quote *Daddy* by heart and believes that 'Daddy' is Ted Hughes. "Ted was a real prick," she says. She hasn't read anything by Hughes.

Pearl, who is in my Creative Writing Class, and who writes poems about why we exist or if thought comes before language, has discovered Kafka. In two weeks she has read through the Kafka oeuvre. She says, "Kafka's odd and funny. Mostly he's funny. Not slapstick funny but odd funny. I mean, Gregor as a beetle?"

I ask my students one day if they think reading is on the decline. I say, "How many of you actually go out and buy books or read a book and recommend it to someone else?" About 10 out of 30 hands go up. One is a boy. *Trainspotting, Junky, Fear and Loathing*, these are the books he likes. The girls, who read and buy way more books than the boys, talk about everything from *Angela's Ashes* ("unconventional and complex, very very funny"), to *Catcher in the Rye* ("I walked around believing I was Holden for a week"), to Francesca Lia Block (really popular with fifteen-year-old girls), to *A Suitable Boy*.

In the interest of talking about books, we do *Book Talk*. A small group of students reads the same book and then gets up in front of the class and discusses it for twenty minutes. They do an author bio, a summary and then they're supposed to debate the book's merits and faults. Two girls have great fun with *Bridget Jones' Diary*. They find it funny, charming and easy to relate to. They like the fact that Bridget is overweight and a slob. They liked the movie too. (Everything in literature class comes back to movies.)

Another group does *The Divine Secrets of the Ya-Ya Sisterhood.* Two girls hate it because its style is flat: "Sidda went to the store. Sidda heard the dial tone. Sidda stood frozen in place." The other two girls love it. The characters are real, the story works.

Three boys talk about *Deliverance* by James Dickey. "An awful book," Carlos says, "The main guy, the guy who tells the story? He's gotta be gay. He goes on this canoe trip with Lewis and he's always admiring Lewis's body, looking at him like he loves him. Anyways, the story was boring and drawn out. Way too descriptive."

Six other boys do *American Psycho*. They admire it. Donald says, "It's kind of funny, you know? You wouldn't think it could be but Bateman loves his clothes and his looks and he spends a lot of time at his appearance and making sure he has all the right stuff on and then he goes out and kills someone. That's kind of funny."

And finally, three girls talk about *First Love* by Turgenev and they hate it. "I mean, look," Erika, one of the presenters, says, "This girl, Zinaida, sleeps with the father of the sixteen-year-old narrator. She's a slut."

I get mad at them. Tell them it's one of my favourite books. I say, "You think all girls who are a bit weird or loose in their sexual choices are sluts. Julia in *1984*, Jill in *Equus*, and now Zinaida."

"Yeah, so what?" their faces say.

I shake my head and roll my eyes. What I want to say is that I'm throwing pearls before swine or that they aren't smart enough, or that they're too lazy or too young to get it. I want those three girls to see the subtlety of the writing, to appreciate Turgenev's style. Instead, I say, "Don't just see a slut. That's pointless," and I tell them to sit down.

Still, it amazes me how many of these kids read, talk about, beg, borrow and buy books. And they've got their opinions. Oh, yes.

Jennifer, on *Alice in Wonderland:* "Too weird. The old man was on opium when he wrote this."

Michelle, on *Alice in Wonderland:* "What a great book. I loved the dream images."

Tamara, on *Dangerous Angels* by Francesca Lia Block: "This is amazing. The best book I've ever read. She's an amazing writer. I love her characters."

Beth, on *The Perks of Being a Wallflower:* "My favourite. Absolutely. It's a Salinger ripoff but a pretty good one."

Colton, on *Requiem for a Dream:* "Anything with drugs, man. That's what I like. I mean, the writing has to be good, but if it's about drugs, I'll read it. *Requiem for a Dream* was the best. And the movie? It was amazing."

And, so on.

These days, in English, we're doing *Othello*. I tell the kids that it's an easy play. It's about betrayal and friendship. About boredom, too. Iago is bored. He's a great character and the play is linear and quick and full of action. There's not a lot of description, I say. And later, of course, we'll watch the movie.

A REALLY FINE DAY
Pamela Lockman

I n my old life, teaching at North Hollywood High School in Los Angeles, I had days when I would walk out of school with my friend Tony and we would be laughing out loud and saying to each other, "Can you believe we actually get paid for this?!" It's true. I even wrote a poem about times like that. And, I am happy to say, I still have days like that. This is about one such day.

At 8 a.m., a full hour before our first class starts, my colleague Ray and I are discussing *Clara Callan*, which my book club just debated the evening before, and which Ray has recently finished reading. I still can't figure out why it got the Governor General's award and the Giller; wasn't *The Stone Carvers* on the same short list? Ray wants me to look at a few pages of *Atonement*. I read and am taken in by the beauty of language, the voice, the detail, the shifts in tone. We are excited about the possibilities for using even this small segment with Advanced Placement students looking at style analysis. A few more paragraphs and now I really want to read the book!

The bell rings and I'm late for homeroom, which also happens to be the Grade 12 class that I will meet again later in the day. Once there, I gush about possible book choices for their upcoming "major paper." The students are gone before long and my first class pours in.

This is Grade 11 and we're on our final day of discussion of Robertson Davies' *Fifth Business*. A student asks, "Can we talk about something that's not on our assignment sheet? How and why did Dunny get interested in saints to begin with?" And we're off. Eight or ten hands immediately go up and before the bell rings again, almost everyone in the class has contributed to our group-think. Conversation ranges from mysticism to religion to

Jungian psychoanalytic theory (He was looking for something—he was no good at magic, but saints are somehow connected to magic, to religion, to miracles…). When I ask for a final evaluation of this book, the verdict is overwhelmingly positive. Students recall the discussions about religion and archetypes as some of the most interesting they've had around a novel. This is a terrific book for students of this age; they're interested in most (if not all) of the things Davies deals with and they're amazingly open about discussing their own beliefs and values.

Luckily, I get to breathe before the next class arrives. They're my Grade 10s, and a grand, rowdy bunch they are! We've recently finished reading and discussing Margaret Atwood's *Cat's Eye*, which the boys, at first, were certain contained nothing for them. However, it didn't take too many class discussions to convince them otherwise. The greatest moment of truth came when one young gentleman suggested, "But girls never *really* act like that…" The males in our room were quite amazed when every girl in the class responded at once that the book has a certain realism to it. On this particular day, as a follow-up to the novel, students have brought examples of what they consider to be "good" art and "bad" art. There is great excitement and much challenging of each others perceptions. Impossible to keep (and not really *wanting* to keep) the noise level down, I have to close the door. I'm often tickled by the sureness of young people. ("This is *definitely* bad art! My baby *sister* could do that! The artist is *stoo-pid!*")

The boys seem to agree: Good Art = Monet, Michelangelo, Leonardo, just about anything old. Bad Art = Rothko, Pollack, just about anything abstract. The girls are a little more open-minded, but are not convinced that Pollack is anything more than a clever fraud. We've gotten a bad batch of books; most of them are falling apart and the printer has offered to replace any that we return. I thought they'd be happy to turn in their scraggly copies, but few do. Most don't want to give up the books they've written all their notes in. Before the bell rings, I circulate some of my favourite marbles, including a few cat's eyes, from my (okay, my stepson's) collection. "Let's start a marbles club!" one boy yells as he walks out the door.

Grade 8 is next. They're wildly energetic and enthusiastic by nature (and hormones!), and today we're continuing presentations of "found

"Bookworm" by Bob Haverluck

chapters." Groups of three or four have written original new material for *The Hobbit*, with which they are all in love. Each piece is three to five typed pages, imitates Tolkien's style, uses his characters, and includes at least four lines of original song. Today's group reads aloud and the rest of the class is more attentive than usual. Who would imagine that 12 and 13 year-olds could sound so much like Tolkien? Sitting there reading to their peers they seem so mature, so much older, and then they get to the song. Leaping out of their chairs and dancing around to the beat of their elvish tune, they bring the house down! We all stomp and chant along, and once more I think, too late, that perhaps the door should be closed.

This is one of those ethereal days when I get to breathe and think and talk literature just about every moment. I spend lunch with a 10th grader who feels that he is not "getting" enough from his reading. He wants help in figuring out meanings beyond the literal and obvious. We talk about some of the recurring motifs and symbols in *Cat's Eye*, and I suggest some strategies for recognizing those in other works. He smiles and thanks me, then I thank *him* for asking. I tell him honestly that I really enjoy these one-on-one discussions and invite him back anytime.

After lunch, my hardest class of the day: double Grade 12. I have been torturing them with Faulkner's *The Sound and the Fury*, not an "easy" read for anyone. We sit in a circle so no one can hide. We continue our discussion of the time- and-Caddy-obsessed, and doomed, Quentin. We look at Macbeth's "Tomorrow and tomorrow and tomorrow" soliloquy once again, and something starts to click. "Life's but a walking shadow..." Students find segments to read aloud. I urge them on. They're getting it! Frustration eases and excitement rises. As we continue to re-read and understand Macbeth's speech, we begin to understand the depths of Quentin's despair and his decision to commit suicide. How sad! How terribly depressing! But this is not us; this is Quentin. "This is one messed up family!" is how more than one of my students put it. Two days ago I thought that maybe I'd made a mistake with this novel, that maybe I'd replace it with something less challenging next year. Today I've changed my mind.

Four o'clock comes quickly. I've spent a fruitless 45 minutes searching the net for the Shirley Jackson story "Charles," which I'm sure my Grade 8s will enjoy. I ask my colleague who's on his way out if he might know where I can find a copy. Within 30 seconds, he produces it from among well over 100 books on his office shelves. Ahhhhhh, life is sweet.

"THAT GUY IS MEN-TAL!"

Sharon Selby

Teaching Shakespeare can be a rather daunting task. I have found that groans and glazed eyes typically greet my enthusiasm for the Bard. I am still rendered speechless when students demand indignantly, "Why can't he just say it in English?" When studying Hamlet, I find myself waiting with morbid anticipation for the kid whose analysis of the play inevitably consists of, "That guy is MEN-TAL!" However, something different happened the last time I started *Macbeth*. When my Grade 11s asked if they had to write another boring essay, I replied, "No, you're going to perform it." I had no idea they would take me seriously.

We read the play together in class. With the prospect of a performance at the end of the unit, everyone paid attention. We discussed character development and motivation, analyzed relationships, and debated tone, innuendo, and word choice. As a class, we developed several different themes and voted on the ones we would emphasize in our rendition. We issued invitations to several classes and grades in the school—this was to be a public performance. We managed a thorough analysis of the text in record time: everyone was anxious to get to the drama but no one wanted to look ridiculous in front of the audience.

Once everyone had a handle on the play itself, we voted on two or three of the most significant scenes from each act. Parts were distributed and the rules were established. Everyone was required to perform at least three speaking parts. Each actor was responsible for translating his or her lines into modem English—I had everything from line-by-line translations to rap (which was actually excellent). Speeches could be shortened as long as significance was not diminished and coherence was maintained.

Nothing else was sacred. For the sake of the audience, we had a narrator who linked the scenes and filled in the blanks. The costume for each character remained the same, but the actors were always switching which resulted in some very interesting cross-gender performances. For example, in one scene Lady Macbeth was played by a genteel girl with a flair for the dramatic; in the next, our star hockey player (wearing a black negligee and sporting a goatee) was wailing in a falsetto and stealing the show.

We called our performance McBeth, a sort of fast-food version of Shakespeare. Our ghostly dagger dangled at the end of a fishing pole. We banged coconut halves (in true Monty Python fashion) to simulate the sound of horses approaching, and we lifted the swords from the Social Studies room for the battles. Our murderers hid behind a single tree branch that they held in front of their faces while they spoke. In the final scene, Macbeth's expression of open-mouthed shock and agony (the actor was draped in a sheet, clutching Macduff's sword to create the illusion of headlessness) had our audience in hysterics. And, because humour was obviously one of the themes we chose to incorporate, we included the gatekeeper scene. The Grade 7 and 8 students were shocked and delighted when the gatekeeper (played by our genteel Lady Macbeth) explained how drink confounded "him" and how "he" exacted his revenge by "peeing and puking like you wouldn't believe." What can I say? It's all in there. That's Shakespeare, kiddies.

In the end, I had to admit our performance was a huge success. *I* had fun! The students had a great time putting our play together, and everyone received marks based on their participation and the quality of their translation. There were also essay questions on the final exam which required that the students identify quotes from the play, and elaborate on their significance in the context of the scene and in the play as a whole. The marks on the final exam were, on average, 10 percent higher than the regular term marks, which demonstrated the academic merit of the project. Younger students even claimed to be looking forward to Shakespeare. I am choosing to believe them.

AN EXAMINATION OF ANOTHER KIND

Joshua J.M. Grummett

with contributions from Jennifer Doran, Larissa Scrimshaw, Gillian
Andrewshenko, Senior 3 students at John Taylor Collegiate, in Winnipeg.
All boldtype sections are excerpts from Manitoba Provincial Senior 4
English Language Arts Standards Exam, June 2002.

Activating Your Thoughts

Consider the following expressions about time. In the space below,
jot down ideas, thoughts, feelings, or experiences that you associate
with them.

My mind had been churning like a cauldron on the boil ever since I
had come into the exam five minutes late. My thoughts were already
'activated'—heck, they were activated enough to provide electricity to a
small South Pacific island. And I was certainly not about to do any 'jotting';
this was the final exam of the Grade 12 English course I'd been taking for
the past four months. I was here to write.

The platitudes and cliches beneath that astounding exam-opening
paragraph didn't help, either. "Time is on your side." "You're running out
of time." "Time flies." This was supposed to be the exit exam, the all-
important one that was indicative of your skill with the English language
at graduation. Reading this first page and realizing that the authors
assumed that I was born yesterday and needed a switch for my brain did
not engender the impression that this was to be taken seriously.

So, I activated, and I jotted, and I waited for the other students to
finish activating and jotting before we all could move on to the much-
anticipated second page.

Reading and Viewing Texts

Read and view the following pages (6-23). While you read, jot down in
the margins any ideas, questions, comments, or reactions you have, and

highlight sections you find important or interesting. You will share your ideas with others later.

Now, this was beginning to annoy me. I was itching to move on to my process piece, the crafting of which would need some time. And here this booklet was peppering me with lovely little pictures and snippets of literature, with the admirable intent of giving me some understanding of the concept of 'Time'. I had a watch. I had wasted too much time before leaving and was late for the exam. I understood time.

Another thing: why do they want to know any 'ideas, questions, comments, or reactions' of mine? There's nothing indicating that this is for marks—these are splash pages intended to get me thinking about time, not to induce me into scribbling in the margins about my watches, clocks and halitosis.

I scanned the two splash pages for anything of interest (after all, it would not do to leave the page blank when it was suggested that I highlight things for later use), when something caught my eye. On the right page, in the upper right-hand corner, there were two stanzas of a poem by Emily Dickinson.

Because I could not stop Death,
He kindly stopped for me;
The carriage held but just ourselves
And Immortality.

We slowly drove, he knew no haste
And I had put away
My labor, and my leisure too,
For his civility.

What I had stubbed my eyes on was the misprint in the first line of the poem; the line actually ran "Because I could not stop for Death,". We had not read this during the course, but I recalled it from a Grade 7 English class; our teacher had written the first two lines as a whole sentence, to demonstrate how starting a sentence with the word 'Because' was done.

READ THIS!

One of the more profound pieces of poetry by an enduring female poet, and the authors of an English exam couldn't even quote it correctly?

I looked at the rest of the splash page. There was an illustration of Canada's time zones, a Dilbert cartoon, an early nineteenth-century French sundial, a diagram of a mechanical watch, the phrase "Carpe Diem! ('Seize the day!')" and a passage from *Ecclesiastes*. The left page yielded a photo of Canadian speed skater Catriona LeMay-Doane, an Aztec calendar, the 'stitch in time saves nine' proverb, a clockbased statue and the first three lines of the soliloquy that Macbeth gives when he hears of the death of his wife.

All told, there were two 'texts' that I had studied before in an English course (one, only coincidentally), and one 'text' that I had studied in middle school Social Studies. I will admit, the authors of the exam had done an impressive job of showing me things that would get me thinking about time. They had in the process left out almost everything that constitutes English literature.

In the Manitoba ELA curriculum, 'text' and 'reading' are defined as follows:

> Text refers to all language forms that can be experienced, discussed, and analyzed. These include print texts, oral texts such as storytelling, dialogues, speeches, and conversations, and visual texts such as pictures, diagrams, tableaux, mime, and non-verbal communication.

> "Reading refers to constructing meaning from texts of any kind."

The product of these definitions was flamboyantly splashed across those two pages of the exam. They gave me a mosaic of photographs, captions, images and mere snippets of better-known pieces of literature. I was given no audio 'texts', and barely any print texts (although, one must wonder about the meaning of 'print texts' now, as both words and images were printed on the page). This struck me as somehow wrong; a semester of my life spent learning the higher forms of English, reading novels, short stories, articles—by authors people recognize, like Sophocles, Brontë, Blake and Shakespeare—and I'm given *pictures* on the exam?

That last phrase in the definition of text is what most threatens the integrity of ELA: "Non-verbal communication." That phrase opens wide the floodgates of the material in a course on English: suddenly, we're talking about studying artwork, mimes and voicemail messages along with Blake, Orwell and Solzhenitsyn. There is a reason that subjects such as Art, Drama and Psychology exist separately from English in the high school curriculum—they are *different fields of study*—interrelated only to an extent, and it is only to that extent that they are incorporated into our study of literature.

And the thought looming large in my mind now is that this is what Senior 4 students are expected to know, leaving high school. Not anything of value, nothing on the large body of English literature, just a skimming off the top of interesting little facts.

I wonder what the faces of my co-workers will be like, 30 years from now, if I recited Shakespeare's 27th sonnet without a single mistake, as I can now. "When in disgrace with Fortune and men's eyes…"

Right above the 'stitch in time saves nine' proverb on the left splash page, there was an image of quarter-notes and eighth-notes in percussion style. It was not written as part of a stave, but along a line, meaning that this extremely simple beat was intended for simple percussion instruments such as tambourine or bongo. Also, I could infer that this was in 2/4 musical time—the first measure yielded two quarter notes, and did not appear to be a pick-up introduction. I realized all this while looking at it, figuring out in the process that the studying I did for my Royal Conservatory exam on music theory must have sunk in more than I'd thought at the time. I also realized that I was probably one of the few students in the room who could glean that from an otherwise esoteric image of circles and lines.

One of the Fundamentals of the English Language Arts Curriculum in Manitoba is "Importance of Prior Knowledge." A brilliant thing to have on paper, as prior knowledge is usually what brings home the bacon, which it did in my case; without all that study of musical principles, I would not have been able to attach any importance to that 2/4 percussion graphic. However, I can't help but wonder what the other students in the room who *aren't* as musical as I am would make of that. Would they just gloss over it?

Would their minds skid to a halt as they tried to puzzle it out, thus preventing them from getting an adequate amount of work done on the other questions? My prior knowledge of fields other than English saved me, in that respect, thus making it quite important: however, if I had studied before the exam (as I am rarely wont to do). I would not have thought to go over music theory. I would have studied old essays and assignments, and gone over one or two with my teacher. Prior knowledge is great, if you know how use it.

After the splash pages came the articles, and here was when I thought, "Finally, I'm getting to actual *reading material.* Done with the introductory chaff." Past English exams were similar to that in layout; there were a few little things to introduce the 'theme' of the exam, and then we moved on to readings that related to what had been taught previously in the course. I remembered, with particular fondness, the year a Bradbury story was included in the readings.

Slow Down! (What's the Rush?)
Andrew Scott

Ten days. Yikes, I've only got 10 days to write this article on rushing. I don't know if I can finish it by then. I need to do a bunch of interviews right away. Maybe a trend watcher can see why we rush—no. maybe a physician or psychologist can say how racing around day after day affects body and soul. And where will I find the people who're rushed? Will they be too busy to talk to me? Oh, boy. This could be tough.

Scott, here, is using shortened sentences to create the impression of rushing. Cool. We took something of the reverse of that in the first poetry unit, how longer lines will make the reader read faster, and short lines will drag out the reader's perception. At least Scott has slowed down to standard newspaper article pacing later on. Now, what other reading material is presented…?

I started scanning the article to glean the salient points before I went back to read it in full, but again my eyes stubbed on something on the page.

> Experts predict that by 2005
> approximately 75 per cent of
> households will have Internet
> access—with 75 per cent desiring
> high-speed connection @home.

The article itself was in a monospaced font similar to Courier, roughly 14-pt in size: this little snippet was quite literally that small on the page, in that size of a block, inset into the left column on the third page of the article. Reading this, I was struck by the impression that the Manitoba ELA curriculum had sold out, beginning to advertise in the exams. (Or Andrew Scott did.) A few years before the exam, "shaw @home" had been the name behind a company selling high-speed Internet connections to middle-class families; seeing something similar crop up in an exam did not set my mind at ease. And furthermore, the article itself makes little mention of the Internet—a demonstration of a search engine in the rushed introduction and the inclusion of e-mail in a list of things that 'call out for an instantaneous response'. This weird little block had barely anything to do with the article into which it was crammed.

Continuing to flip through the booklet, I again stopped on the pages after 'Slow Down!' These pages contained two pieces of artwork; Salvador Dali's *The Persistence of Memory* and a parody of Dali's work called *The Crunch*, by Globe and Mail artist Kagan McLeod. This was brilliant. The only Fine Art which I am reasonably well-versed in is music and music theory, and here I'm being tested on artwork. Great.

Next.

> *The Hornbooks of Rita K*
> Robert Kroetsch
>
> [hornbook #39]
>
> As a small child I was puzzled by clocks. I studied the face of the large clock mounted on the wall in our kitchen, and I tried to understand how adults looked at that face and then said to each other: The train is late today...

READ THIS!

I was lost. What the heck was a 'hornbook'? I had been taught the plot structure of short stories and novels, the different points of rising and falling action in Grecian, Elizabethan and modern plays. I had read plays, short stories, articles and novels. 'Hornbook' was nowhere in my notes. And this piece is only two paragraphs. Lovely.

Next.

> ### Temporal Behaviors
> Carel Germain
>
> Time, like physical and spatial aspects, is an important dimension of both physical and social settings. It takes time to grow and develop, and it takes time to learn. One must have time for solitude and time for interaction, as well as time to develop ways of coping with stress.

Alright, that piece is somewhat thick with simple concepts in sophisticated language, as well as things that I already know. The two balance out—I don't have to read it particularly closely.

Next.

> ### The Funnel
> Anne Szurnigalski
>
> There was once a young girl who was very good with her needle. That is to say, she could make almost anything her mother suggested—providing she had the proper materials, of course.

Hey, cool, a fairy tale. Something that actually might have some vague sort of lasting literary value, if it weren't so contemporary. Note to self: read between the lines, here. Often, the language and superficial events in fairy tales are one huge metaphor for the moral occasionally revealed at the end.

Next.

Procrastination
Bill Carr

I'm here today to confirm the rumours. What people have been saying about me is true. I've come forward on behalf of thousands of others to tell our story. I am a procrastinator.

A lighthearted piece, less than a page long, regarding procrastination. With no discernible form. Or purpose. Just use of the English language. In a humourous way. What am I supposed to glean from this?

Next.

time changes
Duncan Mercredi

at times
late at night
just don't want to close my eyes
fighting off sleep and the next day
daring time to stand still
the ticking of the clock slowing
to match my heartbeat...

This is evoking a good, subtle picture. Not bad poetry. And the time theme here, while somewhat superficial, also requires some deeper thought—sure, he's talking about the dead hours of the morning, but what does he mean?

Next.

Busy Is Best
Jane Stewart

It's not unusual for today's teens to juggle school, part-time work, and an extracurricular activity that may involve an hour or more, a few nights a week.

Add another 20 minutes of homework per class a night and there aren't many hours left in the day.

Sure, balancing homework, jobs, and extracurricular stuff can be a challenge, but there are a lot of benefits, too.

Through how many years of university did Stewart go? For that matter, does she even have an offspring in his or her late teens? I work at Safeway, with two to five four-hour shifts weekly. I'm in two or three different choirs, one of which requires my egress to another high school for two hours every Wednesday. I have weekly piano / singing / music theory lessons. Our school is staging *Joseph and the Amazing Technicolor Dreamcoat*, and in that I have two lead roles: that requires my lunch hours and two to four hours after school every week. I manage to keep my weekends mostly free for homework and recreation, and I get roughly seven to eight hours of sleep an evening. This should not be possible, but it is, and it's nothing new.

I'll go back to this piece of elegant craftsmanship when I approach the exam questions.

Next.

Recording Ideas From the Text

1. Comment on the ideas about time from the visual and print texts you considered most interesting.
2. Formulate a question about time that you would like to share with others in your group.

I drew a blank. I had only found two out of the seven texts provided for my viewing pleasure interesting enough to go back and read in full. And the prompt they're giving me is vague. Am I to comment on the *ideas* that I found most interesting or on the texts that I found most interesting?

On reading the second question, I was quite tempted to blurt out with one of Gollum's riddles from Tolkien's *A Hobbit*: "This thing all things devours: birds, beasts, trees, flowers; gnaws iron, bites steel; grinds hard stones to meal; slays kings, ruins towns, and beats high mountain down."

I then realized that nobody would get it, it would be quite rude to do in the first place, and no one wanted me to flaunt my frightening memory skills anyway. So I recorded ideas from the texts and prepared a question for my group: "How did corporeal, materialistic, mortal beings come up with an intangible, lasting concept, such as time, prove that it existed, and then go on to structure their lives around it?"

Clarifying Thoughts With Others

Discuss with your group:
- Initial thoughts on the subject. (See Activating Your Thoughts, page 5.)
- Ideas gathered from the written or visual texts. (See Recording Ideas from the Texts, page 24.)
- Question(s) you have formulated. (See Recording Ideas from the Texts, previous page.)

Record ideas from your group discussion below.

For the first 30 seconds of this group discussion, we stared at each other like wary animals. Dead silence reigned. I could almost hear the faint footfalls of tumbleweed ghosting by behind me, if tumbleweed were to exist in the library of a suburban high school.

Thankfully, Kevin, a classmate of mine, broke the silence. "So. Josh, what did you get for…"

As I shared my rather unorthodox views of time (much of which had very little to do with what the reading material mentioned). The 20 minutes were spent unremarkably, with myself holding forth on what I perceived time to be, and the other members of my group writing and asking me the odd question.

I don't know whether or not this was the case with other groups; there were some tables at which there was almost no speech, while other groups were talking amongst themselves excitedly, filling the air with vibrant musings and the sounds of swift writing.

I just know that I would have been more focused and better able to work on my own.

When the time allotted for the group discussion passed, we returned to our previous seats (if we had moved), and flipped to the next page of the exam booklet.

Connecting Ideas
1. After considering ideas about time in this Process Booklet explain how your own view of time has or has not changed since childhood.

How has my view of time changed since childhood? Well, first off, a more effective question would ask how my view of time has changed since perusing the material included for enjoyment, but I'm not taking this exam to critique it.

The main reason that people segregate their early lives into infancy, childhood, adolescence and, finally, adulthood is that these segregations encompass a change in thought, world perception and time. An infant is as different from a young child as that child is from a teenager, and as different as the teenager is from an adult. These differences are not only physical, but mental.

An infant has almost no perception of time. It wakes, it cries, it is fed, it goes to sleep. It is taken out in strollers and in arms to experience the tangible aspects of the world, not the intangible aspects. So time means nothing to an infant.

A young child, on the other hand, finds himself on his own two feet, in regards to time. In kindergarten or first grade, he is taught how to read clocks, both analog and digital. His parents nag him out of the door in a general schoolward direction when the clocks say "8:15"; he rushes out of school with his classmates when the clocks say "3:30." He learns that adults rely on these clocks to tell them when to do things, and the first steps towards his understanding of time are taken.

A teenager lives by the clock. Her lunchtime choir class is at 12:20, but she has a double-spare beforehand, ranging from 9:38 to 12:04. With a half-hour of homework each for Biology, Psychology, Math, and English, this gives her just enough time to complete said homework, rush down to the cafeteria to grab a lunch (today's special being Full Poutine and Coke, and

the cafeteria lady makes amazing poutine), and talk to Emilia about that
bush party that's supposed to happen on Friday.

As I have moved from childhood to adolescence (at least) in my perceptions,
thought and sense of time, it is safe to say that my perception of time has
changed through maturity.

I left out the tangential thoughts in parentheses when I answered the
question, but otherwise it ran much the same. I found that I had to cater
to the expectations of the exam authors: I needed my brain to be switched
on and off, my memory refreshed periodically, and my self esteem boosted
through questions that asked about my feelings more than they tested my
knowledge of English.

In the curriculum, there exist a number of things called "General
Learning Outcomes"—a set of goals for student performance. They all look
good on paper, but one of them strikes me as particularly odd in its turn
of phrase.

General Learning Outcome 2

Students will listen, speak, read, write, view, and represent to
comprehend and respond personally and critically to oral, print,
and media texts.

The curriculum wants students to respond *personally* to texts. I have
never been one to rave about how *Hamlet* brought me in touch with my
'young rebel' side or how *Wuthering Heights* gave me a new perspective on
a past relationship of mine. I will gladly tell of my opinions on anything
under the sun, but to have to describe how I feel about something for an
exam would be like tacking butterflies to cardboard.

What's more, my purpose in learning advanced English is not to have
my teacher validate my feelings. I am taking advanced English to learn how
to communicate in all uses of the English language, from sonnets to
stream-of-consciousness. Sir Isaac Newton was a scientist, first and
foremost, but he still had the skills to write his *Principia* in an exact and
legible manner. How I feel about any particular piece of work doesn't
matter: what matters is whether or not I have understood what the author
was trying to communicate, the ways in which he or she did it and my

mastery of those methods of communication. Teaching me the skills to respond critically about something is what I need. How I feel doesn't enter into it.

The second question went by without much ado; it began with the word "Examine." That made my job all the swifter, and I sat back and ruminated while the time allotted for Connecting Ideas passed by.

After that came the Reading Response questions, the period of the exam where we were to be tested on how well we could communicate our reactions and thoughts on the pieces we had just read. (Personally, I was hoping that all the questions would prompt me to "Analyze," "Examine," or "Identify." By taking the exam, I was required to give correct answers, and any questions on how I felt about any of the pieces would seal my fate.)

Only one question stands out particularly in my mind from the Reading Response section of the exam.

HORNBOOK #39

5. Analyze how "Hornbook #39" does or does not show that our society teaches children to live by the clock.

Now, as an all-encompassing axiomatic rule of thumb, exams are positive. This means that whenever a "does or does not" clause shows up in a question (as it does in this one), the student is supposed to answer that it does do this and that. Nobody wants to hear about how such-and-such didn't do something, or that so-and-so failed to come through on something else. We get that in the news all the time.

But the thing was, "Hornbook #39" did *not* show that our society teaches children to live by the clock. "Hornbook #39" was two paragraphs in length. The first paragraph told, from a child's perspective, about adults living by the clock. The second paragraph delineated the child's confusion about this. Nothing more. Nothing less. To answer in the manner that the examiners expected was impossible; to answer in the manner that honesty required would bring many unhappy returns. "Hornbook #39" did not show how our society teaches children to live by the clock, it only showed *that* they learn to live by the clock. So I did what I typically do in such situations: I sat on the fence.

I analyzed how "Hornbook #39" did not show that our society teaches children to live by the clock. I analyzed it to death; I even went down to sentence structure and idiom use as to how it did not show that our society teaches children to live by the clock. And after I'd proved all that, I went back on everything and stated that *if it did* show that our society teaches children to live by the clock, here's how it would be done.

I'm fairly confident that this was a good answer, given our society's penchant for democracy and double standards.

The next page yielded a description of the process by which we were to write our process piece.

Writing Task

Before you begin planning and drafting your texts, consider
- our personal relationship with time
- how time makes an impact on lives
- how perceptions of time change
- the role of time through history
- perceptions of time in different cultures
- your own questions, discussions, and reflections

Writing Task:

In a written text to share with others, develop an idea or impression about time that you consider important or interesting.

Well, as far as I know, "Slow Down!" covered our personal relationship with time and how time makes an impact on lives; "Hornbook #39" discussed how perceptions of time change: "Temporal Behaviors" delineated the role of time through history and perceptions of time in different cultures. This leaves me with my own questions, discussions and reflections—plagiarism is bad practice.

Slim pickings, since my mind was only activated this morning.

READ THIS!

Determine:
- the central idea
- the purpose
- the audience (must be public, not personal)
- the context (the situation in which your audience will experience the text)
- the form

You may choose your own written form, or select or adapt one of the following:

- persuasive essay
- column
- interview
- poem
- memoir
- short story
- radio screen/TV/stage script
- eulogy
- speech

In making your selection, be aware that you will have three days to develop your text.

We went over the first six items in class; those became integral to every piece we wrote. No surprise there. But what's with the forms? The specialization of the essay is somewhat understandable, as not every essay is persuasive; some are expository, some are merely dissertations on a subject. The interview, poem, memoir, short story, eulogy and speech we covered in class. They could have saved space by writing 'dramatic script' instead of listing the places where scripts are used. And what the heck did they mean by column? Surely not a Corinthian pillar as my 'text'? Or do I leave three-inch margins on either side of what I write? There was an unspoken assumption that "column," in this context, referred to a newspaper or magazine column, but the initial vagueness and lack of specificity here is not helpful.

At least they're being generous enough to let me research overnight. I may not be able to take any outside materials into the exam, but I can borrow materials from the library or look things up on the Net and have them fresh in my mind for tomorrow morning.

The bell rang, the teachers spake forth in clarion calls on how to pack up and we filed out of the library like sand through the hourglass. The remainder of the process writing went without further ado, as it was fairly straightforward: I put down my form as 'editorial,' and I wrote about how George W. Bush has only so much time before the next election, hence his war with Iraq, his repeated bills, etc. But the questions at the end bothered me.

Reflecting

1. Publishers and presenters enhance a text with features such as visuals, layout, pacing, props, and sound effects. If you were to publish or present your text, describe a feature you would include and explain how it would enhance your texts for your audience.

I agreed, in that texts were often enhanced. But what does this have to do with English? Again, here the curriculum is bringing in things that have very little to do with the study of English. During the course of the curriculum, we were taught how to communicate through the various uses of English; never once did we discuss enhancing our communication through methods that didn't involve the literary text itself. My 'text' was an editorial; thus, my answer would run something along the lines of the inclusion of the editorial cartoon, in this case, a tense and anxiety-stricken President Bush, sitting at his desk, under a looming clock.

2. Using examples, explain how one of the statements below describes the creation of your written text.

I experimented with a new form or style to enhance communication.

I revised my text to enhance its effectiveness.

This caused me to grin. The process of the exam was such that the actions which the question described—experimenting with a new form or style, or revising the text—left no evidence. The marker on the other side of the exam wouldn't know whether or not the form in which I wrote the process piece was new or not, as "using examples" would mean bringing in some of my old assignments, which was forbidden by the exam. And I had written my rough draft in pencil—thus, all I had to do was change a phrase or two, and I would have my answer supplied for the second statement. I, eventually, answered that the editorial was a new style for me (it wasn't), but I felt that certain freedoms within the editorial would suit aspects of my personality to the point that my communication would be enhanced through the ease in which I would be able to write.

My pen disengaged from the exam booklet with due swiftness. I was done. I would not have to go through this trial again until next May, when I would write the AP English exam. I leaned back in my chair, clasped my hands behind my head, and used the six minutes remaining to count the soundproofing holes in the ceiling panels.

"Knowledge is power." One is quite forcibly prevented from moving in the circles of today's world without it. It is sad that the identity of this person has been lost to history. However, the anonymity of this person is not surprising.

Over the past century, humankind has taken significant leaps and bounds in advancement: 66 years elapsed between the development of flight to the first steps taken on the moon; however, trigonometry, integral to flight, was originated in early Greece and Egypt and has not changed greatly since. These significant leaps and bounds have been made possible by the level of education in the innovators behind them. Would Einstein have gone as far as he did without the skills to write the treatises and essays needed to communicate his ideas? And would we, in a predominantly English speaking society, have the incredible body of literature that we do if the teaching of it were not given a heavy emphasis in the system of education that we use to bring our children from childhood to adulthood?

No, we would not. Admittedly, the development of truly profound literary skills takes time and practice: Shakespeare wrote his greatest plays in the final 12 years of his life, and there are few young authors of note who are not known by the works that they wrote in their later years. Each author whose works have lasted, each author whose work has become part of the body of English literature, had his or her foundation in their education. It is likely safe to say that these foundations were rigid and designed to immerse the student in what was a short list of "approved" authors—book reviews of contemporary authors (of the time) would be discouraged in favour of such classics as *Beowulf,* or Chaucer's *Canterbury Tales,* if not a section of the Bible itself.

In contrast, we have the system of literature education of today. Students in elementary and middle schools are given book review assignments. The focus in these early levels is on getting the student to read and to enjoy reading therefore, they may choose any book he or she likes. The basics of spelling, grammar and articulation in general, are taught at these levels, to give the students the most basic of skills needed to communicate their ideas. This exam made me feel like a sixth-grade student again, testing me on the most basic of skills needed to communicate my ideas.

There were 75 soundproofing holes in the ceiling panel I was gazing at by the time the teacher came to collect my exam, but if these examinations of another kind are to continue, I am not sure how many holes would exist in our education by the time the final examiner comes to collect.

POETRY IN THE SCHOOLS
Di Brandt

I spent five happy years during the 1990s in the Manitoba Artists-in-the-Schools program, visiting high school English classes and conducting weeklong poetry writing workshops with students and teacher. I found that both teachers and students were often nervous when I first arrived about not having studied very much poetry, and about what would be expected of them in the workshop. Sometimes they would be mumbling something apologetic about image and metaphor and iambic pentameter, trying to remember what the technical definitions of those terms were. So I usually began by involving them in very simple rhythmic chants by well known Canadian poets like Bill Bissett, Paul Dutton, Robert Priest, Penn Kemp and Lillian Allen, to loosen up the atmosphere and to undercut the fear of poetry which is so endemic to this culture (sometimes I have it too). I pointed out that rhythm is the underlying principle of poetry, and that it is a very simple and profound aspect of language which every little child understands from a very early age, even before learning to speak. (Researchers are now saying that babies respond to rhythm and sound and tone of voice even before they're born.) I talked about the basic elements of rhythm: repetition and sound. (And pleasure!) I encouraged them to perform the chants in groups, antiphonally, sometimes performing them with accompanying rhythm instruments and creative movement.

After we'd firmly established an atmosphere of creative play, I read them other vibrant examples of contemporary Canadian poetry, focussing on particular features such as an innovative use of memory, or sound, or voice, or spacing. I brought dozens of collections of poetry along to pass around. I found students were extremely interested in browsing through these collections, often hunting through them for particularly intriguing or titillating bits and pointing them out surreptitiously to their neighbours (to my secret delight). I gave them numerous models to work from, from concrete to dada to philosophical meditations. I found that it was easy to stimulate extremely interesting writing by just reading and very briefly discussing a few poems in this fashion and then asking the students to write something on the spot, inspired by the examples. I also found it easy, in this way, to introduce them to a wide range of fairly sophisticated poetry which they might otherwise have felt intimidated by as listeners and readers.

Students often produced a range of amazing, playful, emotionally engaging and even formally complex poems over the course of the week. One of the great delights of the workshop was discovering that often it was the students who had trouble with the regular curriculum, whether from boredom or lack of concentration or literacy skills, that wrote the most interesting, daring and innovative poetry. I often discussed this remarkable fact with the teacher afterward: it seemed that poetry unlocked for many of the marginalized students a language that made sense to them, that enabled them to be creative and articulate.

This phenomenon was most apparent in the core area schools, where students often came to class in desperate circumstances. One class I visited had recently suffered a suicide, and several students came in stoned. It was impossible in those circumstances to think about math or chemistry, but reading poetry with them and then giving them permission to write it unlocked eloquent streams of language in the students. Many wrote about their absent fathers or lost loves or about having babies (!)—about the deeply moving experiences of their lives which didn't seem to have a place anywhere else in the curriculum. Most of them would not have written about these subjects if they'd been assigned (and indeed, who would assign them), but because of the magical mediating presence of the poetry, they were able to find formal approaches to their experiences which were profoundly playful and highly communicative, often with a strong performance element to them, which gave us all great delight (and sometimes awe) to witness and experience.

The teachers who chose to participate actively in the workshops also wrote some amazing poems. It was, many of them said, a moment of spiritual replenishment for them, of creative renewal.

Writing poetry is perhaps the best way to teach students (and all of us) to read poetry. Reading poetry is perhaps the most important kind of reading that students can do, because of its capacity to engage us in such profoundly spiritual and emotional ways, keeping our souls alive in this increasingly soulless age, where communication is being reduced to impersonal information-giving, and the ecstatic, imaginative aspect of our lives is being lost. It is after all the language of love, of beauty, of hope, of terror, of despair, the language of connection. Many philosophers have argued that poetry is the language that can save us from dehumanization in a mechanistic age; that it can nurture in us the creative energy we need to face the urgent challenges of our time, particularly the ecological crisis facing us in the coming decades. Jonathon Bate has declared that poetry is the language that will "save the earth," if we practice it enough, because it is our species song, it is how we take our rightful place among the many other living beings that make up our earthly home. I couldn't agree more: we must insist on keeping poetry at the forefront of our educational curricula, and encourage our children to exercise their creative poetic imaginations on a regular basis.

Postscript: I once brought a bag of all the "first books of poetry published in Canada" for the previous year to a class, having recently sat on a jury for the Gerald Lampert Award for "best first book of poetry in Canada." How many books do you think were in that jury pile, I asked the students before hauling out my bags. Two thousand? they said. Five hundred? Forty-five, I replied, and passed them around. How much do you think the prize for best first book of poetry in Canada is worth, I asked. Two hundred thousand? they said. A hundred thousand? Lower, much lower, I said. Fifty thousand, twenty thousand. Lower, I said, much much lower. I wish I could have recorded their faces when we got to the right amount, which was $500, in those days (I think it has doubled since then), the dismay and bewilderment in them. Why do we adults buy so quickly into the logic of poverty when it comes to one of our richest, most valuable, most easily sustainable cultural resources? Let's support poetry in the schools, in the libraries, in the media, in the publishing houses, according it the value our children instinctively understand. Let's give our children a future they can believe in. Let's give them poetry.

ON READING FOR CONTENT

Jan Horner

Be concise for so much depends
on the red wheelbarrow.
Foreign phrases are a pain
in the thesaurus.
As if clear, compact, cogent
was all we ever needed
to keep us alive and moving
sensible, effective & capable of dream.

It was on at the Library first:
Curious George and the yellow hat
and the first words read alone,
"the Cat in the Hat" then off to school
with Dick and Jane and those readers
with bracing names: their flung open windows
high flights and all sails a-set.

Later came those separate books: prince and pauper
both poor little rich boys, then Miss Haversham's plot
amidst her ruined and rotting wedding feast,
and put-upon Pip, you little dickens
a defenseless child and her willing pawn, unlike
Miranda safe on a island where every father would
like to pen his nubile daughter, and Prospero

his library, a dukedom large enough but still
leering Caliban to keep at bay. And Tess, no magician father
could rescue her, shaved eyebrows and digging turnips
the least of her sorrows. Meanwhile Prince Hal stepped
into the breach, transformed from play boy to warrior king
and Lady MacBeth washes her hands, unable to awake
from a dream of witches and forests coming
to take her husband and her bitter crown.

You can be led but what makes you drink.
A trust in your reading, what comes
with practice and slow re-reading
awash in words, all over & sunk in, trusting
your eyes, ears, intuition
letting words taunt and inflame
letting their stress and beat
feed and comfort, draw out some sense
of what you are, and know.
So much more, comes when you
give in, body and soul
words taut and singing, a plucked string
inside, an echo: how you know you are here.
Don't be afraid, everything changes, becomes
something else, my dukedom to a library
and what has been cooking all the while:
your story evolving, the pages turning
in your surrender a little death,
a self forgetting
your youth, absent from felicity awhile
but what foments in you, both rich and strange.

"Woman with her head in a book" by Bob Haverluck

"WHY READ?"

David Welham

W hen I heard that question, my head dropped to the left and then tilted up. I searched the ceiling for an answer. A jumble of possible answers were quickly discarded. I was quite prepared to make a list until I ran out of mental fingers. I wasn't sure what the order would be but I wanted to be sure to say something profound. Yet there was no simple answer, no pronouncement (read soundbite or dust jacket blurb), and no ready quote (although I'm sure someone said it and someone wrote it down). My brain had locked because I might as well have been asked why breathe?

Finally I answered, "Because when you feel alone, you know you're not."

My answer, like any other, has a story behind it. I used the word "story" rather than "reason" because I am a reader. A life with books provided worlds in space, worlds of the past and worlds of ideas that only existed as words on paper. The anticipation of an ending became a yearning that kept me reading under the covers with a flashlight long after I was supposed to be asleep.

In hindsight I wondered what else to say. Would I be preaching to the converted? Therefore, I would merely be strengthening your resolve or making you feel better about yourself. Maybe my purpose is to give you a one liner or an argument for those who ask you the same question but who are really saying why bother?

Moses Znaimer, head of CITY-TV and its spinoff channels, argued that once again Western society has entered a phase when the image has triumphed over the word. Whether that is due to television or advertising or the combination of the two, the image (the visual) is instantly recognizable and therefore accessible and seemingly understandable. Like language development, visual symbols and their manipulation are instinctive, or in computer technology—it's hardwired. Reading, on the other hand, is a skill; it must be practised and therefore, for some, is work. Reading requires more and varied areas of the brain to function because in many ways reading is about translation. The brain compares the words to what has come before, context and what has previously been known—analysis and interpretation. These are the skills of the traditional Literature class.

That's a good thing. The brain, like any other muscle, needs to work. The "use it or lose it" mantra of a fitness guru applies here. Nothing worth having is "fun, fast and easy" for it will never be appreciated. Reading, however, can provide its own buzz; a sensation as physical as the satisfaction of working the body. It is possible to experience the joy of the acquisition of knowledge. If not then why would Trivial Pursuit and other games of lists and stats be popular. Stories, however, are what we are raised on as individuals, as a culture and as a species.

The brain, as it develops from infancy, needs language to help it form; this may explain the baby's ability to babble every sound and then sort out what its culture requires. Reading (to children initially) helps to introduce the brain to language and structure that is not part of everyday conversation or environment. Independent reading introduces additional vocabulary and ideas. Books are like the professional storyteller of the tribe or the clan who came to entertain and instruct; they are even more necessary now that the nuclear family means isolation from many of the evolutionary socializing techniques.

Stranger yet is the development that television and movies (media) have become surrogate storytellers. Unfortunately, TV is a stranger readily given access to the children. True there are good shows for children but even *Sesame Street* uses a model of advertising—rapid shifts and lots of visual hits to remain engaging. (It was designed to sell learning to urban poor—read "black children.") When TV and movies become the only source of story, problems arise. TV is about show and not conclusion. It is possible to see and hear the most profound event or idea on TV but the set (or program) will never tell you to turn it off and go think about what was witnessed, think about how that idea applies to your life or how it could be integrated. Instead it will show an ad for peanut butter or panty liners and then continue the narrative as if the advertisement is part of the story line. And when that show ends another begins.

Hollywood, the world's most influential dream machine doesn't tell very many stories when the basic plot, theme or conclusion is considered. Take, for example, the romance movie. The characters spent the whole movie trying to get together, overcoming whatever obstacles seem to keep them apart—sometimes even their mutual disdain. The conclusion occurs when they come together and presumably live happily ever after. A nice story for a five year old—a sanitized fairy tale. (Certainly not a Grimm's fairy tale). In life, as in literature, that's where the story really begins. A more realistic story for any teen falling in love for the first time is to know that the work of the relationship comes after you get together and in fact continues throughout the relationship. More importantly, you don't always fall in love with the right person.

The other problem with a purely visual world view, taken from television or movies, is that it is created; that is, narrowly defined. More importantly, the question should be: which points of view are left out? When the camera captures what is in front of it, it leaves out the peripheral and rear view. It is a point of view that increasingly panders to only the lowest aspect of the human experience; anything to maintain viewers. Reading provides the chance for real interaction; the "I am" in imagination—the ability to imagine. The ability to create.

A practical example might be *Harry Potter* or *Lord of the Rings*. When the boats approach Hogwarts or the Seige of Helm's Deep occurs, the reader's imagination fills in what has not been described. What does a great castle look like? How big are massive blocks of stone? With a few words, a good writer creates a thousand pictures. That's why when a reader sees a movie adaptation of a book they say often that it wasn't as good as the book. Or it wasn't the same. Perhaps their favorite part has been left out or warped to fit the demands of the screen narrative. It certainly wasn't as good as they imagined it. A non-reader says it was different but the movie was better because now they could see it. The reader has the ability to read

> "Instruction in all six language arts equips students for effective participation in a technological society in which information, communication, arts and entertainment are increasingly conveyed in language forms other than print"(7)

between the lines and to create the worlds of the mind. That's the power of self or, in current jargon, empowerment. As children move from picture books to text-only, they gain another life skill: reading between the lines. Non-readers live a much more literal life, though I prefer the word "concrete" for the metaphor. Not much grows on concrete and nothing gets through. That means that when they listen they don't hear between the lines either. That's why, I suppose, so much of their world has to be in their face or why their humor lacks subtlety. They don't make the connections because they don't have the reference points to make them. Worse yet, from an English teacher's perspective, they don't even have the basic stories from which allusions are made. In practical terms, they are culturally illiterate. Yet all the laws, institutions and forms around them are based on those connections.

The historical example might be the early Christian church. The basic communication of ideas was visual, a set of standard images and poses, in books, glass or painted around the walls and ceilings. A uniformity of vision. The language, Latin, was a code that gave only a few access to the understanding. That's why many elements of pre-Christian religions still existed in the daily life of peasants. By the time of Martin Luther, when the printing press and prosperity created readers who owned a bible they could read for themselves, often in their native language, the problems for the Catholic Church began in earnest. The questioning of authority that the west holds as a basic for democracy truly came into being.

In *1984*, Orwell's major character, Winston Smith, rewrites history while his friend removes words from the dictionary and everyday language.

The reason, he explains, is that the fewer words a person knows, the less they will be able to think. That means that the fewer symbols and ideas a person has the fewer options they have. Only reading provides those options. That seems to be true when I listen to students speak to each other; the best students have a range of language whereas the least academic use one word to describe everything—a movie can be "boring" but so can an exam.

Books provide the range of possibility, not only through vocabulary and information, but also in the ability to see other worlds and world views in a way other mediums do not, cannot or will not. Reading literally allows the reader to see other possibilities and perspectives if not truths.

More importantly, a great book gives the opportunity to actually experience another life. A good friend commented that he would never be an eighty-year-old woman but after reading *The Stone Angel* he knew what it was like to be one.

Joseph Campbell, in *Power of Myths*, was asked, why read myths. He answered, anyone can live a life without them, especially in a technological culture, but there will come a time of crisis when the ancient stories will be the blueprint or software for survival, not physical but psychological and spiritual. In that sense alone, everyone needs a story, perhaps several stories, that define and explain their place in time (age) and circumstance or context. If those stories come only from modem forms of media, then the only option would seem to be to take something buy something or associate yourself with a product or brand name. These are not the things however that satisfy in the long run or that make life meaningful—give it purpose.

If the medium is the message, that message may well be to view our own destruction as entertainment.

Why read literature to find those answers or those directions for your own life? For me, the answer is simple—there are choices. In Hollywood or the latest ad campaign, there is usually only one vision and therefore one voice to tell you who to be or rather what you can be. (It's called fashion.) In any given month all the faces on the magazine covers look remarkably the same.

Literature, writing as an art form like the older form of storytelling, is about possibilities. It is therefore about connections between writer and reader, between past and present and between the internal and the external worlds.

Why read literature? Or what is literature? It is not just something published by Penguin paperbacks but within any genre there are writers who present the human condition. Whether this is the best of Stephen King or Neil Gainman's *Sandman* (a comic book), it is the writing that challenges and pushes the reader that makes it an art form and therefore literature. While everyone needs a junk food read (fast, fun and easy), a steady diet of processed text is as bad as processed food. It satisfies for the moment but provides no nourishment. For tennis players, unless you play against someone better, you never improve or rise to a new level. That's why reading is the quest itself. Once the reader knows that they are on the journey, the more the experience of life is appreciated.

When I read I knew I was not alone because I was reading about some who shared the same life, witnessed it in the same way and who had survived. It also taught me not to fear the silence. I did not need to fill the empty external space with the electronic wallpaper of TV and the blast of music. With a book I could go deep inside the pages and create my own world. The weight of the book in my hands and the smell of the paper— all my senses told me I was home—a place in the physical world to which we can never return.

WHY DO WE NEED BOOKS?

Rhian Brynjolson

W e live in an age saturated with information from multimedia sources. We have a new, 'improved', integrated, cultural literacy. Technology has wedded text, voice, music, graphics in a fast-paced format so that images fly past, keeping us enthralled and constantly entertained. We can scan and scroll, e-mail, cut and paste, and select and delete faster each day. We can continuously watch music videos decorated by tattooed body parts and guns. We can watch sitcoms and movies on 400 channels that tell us abbreviated stories with special effects, full surround soundtracks and actors much more adept at voice, character, martial arts and muscle tone than any teacher, and with the added advantages of lighting, costume, scripts and sets.

Why should we write books, when the market for screenplays is so much more lucrative? Why would we build libraries when information on any subject we can imagine is available, more or less accurately, on the worldwide web? Dodging advertising, we can find the poetry of William Blake, updates from NASA, or a teenager's misinformed web page, equally well. We can chat without the risk of face to face contact, choosing the 'on line' identities that suit us. We can play computer games, defeating enemies, winning levels of achievement and glory, while exploring whole imaginary worlds. As teachers we can photocopy or download excerpts of text for quick reading by our most impatient students.

Why do we still need books? Why would a teacher bother to haul heavy, bound, paper copies of written text into a classroom at the risk of loss, graffiti and overdue library fines, or shop at used book sales spending their own hard-earned cash? There must be some reason—other than great coffee—that bookstores are surviving and teachers are persisting in using these archaic objects with their students.

To begin with, the value of traditional print literacy in a child's educational development need not be pitted against the value of modern multi-media literacy as an either/or proposition. If we state a strong case for the valuing of books in a language arts curriculum, we need not devalue the importance of other forms of literacy. Students should be educated in media literacy and learn skills for critically 'reading' a variety of visual and media texts. Distinguishing sources, deciphering graphs and numerical data, analyzing elements of visual images, developing a critical scepticism to advertising, recognizing slogans and sloppy arguments, and searching for alternative interpretations, are all essential.

However, books play a role in a child's educational development that the electronic media cannot. Books require concentration. Reading a book requires that the reader stay still, focus on one small area of text, exert effort to decode the symbolic markings of print, and observe closely the elements of static illustrations. It is a slow activity. This is no small thing. While electronic media typically provides for the 'reader' something much closer to instant gratification, books are teaching us how to concentrate over an extended period of time. Books teach us how to be in a quiet place where we can use our own inner voice to tell a story. In books, the whole picture is not provided; we are not spoon-fed. Meaning is constructed in the mind of each individual reader, who decodes it from an abstract medium through active imagining. If watching television is a passive pastime, then reading requires active participation. The resulting abilities to concentrate, observe, focus, and critically analyze subtle texts are skills necessary for any discipline, any kind of learning.

For many who study literature, there is also a consensus about quality that does not yet exist in popular culture. The kinds of music, movies, videos or websites that we visit depend on personal preferences and tastes. Multi-media have not existed long enough to gather the same weight of cross-references and rebirth. Yet it is possible to know if some works are better or worse than others if we use the conventions of literature as a standard against which other texts can be measured. We have had centuries of conversation with Shakespeare to revisit, recycle, steal from and innovate

WHY DO WE NEED BOOKS?

with his ideas. We might use popular culture as a *means* to lead reluctant students into encounters with significant texts. We would use the current remakes of *Romeo and Juliet*, for example, to gain enthusiasm for and comprehension of the original plays.

In books we can encounter the source material from which the media text was born. Writing is the first step in the process of developing stand-up comedy, feature length movies, or television sitcoms. We would be selling students short if we did not thoroughly introduce them to the forms necessary for creative processes. In books we have a glimpse, albeit through the editor's rewriting, at encountering the author's original intentions and authentic voice as it exists before the big studio production process takes over. We have access to whole texts, in context, not pulled piecemeal from web sites or photocopiers. Adding our own scribbled notes in the margins, we can revisit favourite passages and build a depth of understanding and a web of reference points that speak to us a decade later. As an aside we might note that books do not contain advertising which may explain why the average income for Canadian writers is so low. The submerged messages and values are conveyed more subtly in books, embedded in language, the narrative and the characters.

Books are beautiful and intimate objects. They were once as valuable as gold, copied by scribes, decorated with hand-drawn illuminations and owned only by the wealthy. Books are still considered valuable enough that we take it for granted that many should be housed in dedicated public buildings where the public has the right to use them freely, under the careful scrutiny of watchful librarians.

The concreteness of written and illustrated books is of special value to young learners who need to hold and manipulate real objects and make tactile connections as they learn. Beginning with literally textural books with fake fur rabbits and scratch-and-sniff cut-outs, preschoolers can find objects and images between the covers of a book that have interest and meaning. As a survival strategy, reading together might get tired families through tired evenings. Cuddled up for bedtime stories told in the intimate voices of family, telling and retelling familiar stories, playing with words and conversing about the text, provides more warmth, more contact, and more human interaction than any form of technological communication.

Rhian Brynjolson

Our children demanded that we read the same books over and over, giggling at the same jokes and memorizing the text until they could recite it back to us, taking their first baby steps as readers.

Books also offer us the visual narrative of illustration and we can 'read' it as it interprets or diverges from the written text. Poring together over familiar illustrations, we can absorb the detail and humour in the artist's drawing. Reading is a sensory experience; we lean against our loved ones, feel the weight of the hard-cover edition of *Alice in Wonderland,* smell the binding and inks, hear the reader's voice, see the richness of illustrations and revisit them like an old and valued friend.

Why do we need books? To learn to concentrate, to think and to imagine. To grapple with big ideas in the wider context of a conversation with a whole culture and to help us mark the growth of our ideas. To study the forms and structures of creative processes. To encounter another person's thoughts with all the depth of subtext and context. To hold a beautiful treasury of stories that helps us to build relationships with our family. To model the art of storytelling, so that we can begin to tell our own stories to each other. As readers, writers, illustrators, parents, teachers and students, we need to value the place of books in our lives and ask our schools to continue to value books as an important part of the education of our children.

LEONARD COHEN: 1

Melanie Cameron

She hasn't touched Leonard Cohen
since the sun fell down
on their dock last summer.
He sits in her room
all of himselves on a shelf
beside one another.
She misses him and that he doesn't
come 'round, doesn't
hum husky lyrics, doesn't
write poetry for her, that he
feeds tea and oranges to Suzanne.

She admits there is a difference
between Jew and Mennonite
between Montreal and Waterloo County
between black hat and persecution
     and black hat and persecution.
She listens when they tell
her he is
older, that he was famous before she was
known to anyone but god. But the man she knows
is 35 is 57 is 21. He lives
a little ahead of her and
they are the same age.

He makes her
keep touching. She keeps touching
his mind each time
she licks her thumb and
turns a page.

CENSORSHIP ISSUE—
OF MICE AND MEN

Sheldon Oberman

I was a first year teacher in a small Manitoba town, glad to be in a close community with strong values. Then I discovered that some of those values were quite different than mine.

I got my lesson on Parent Teacher Night. I glided through the first few interviews feeling like a master teacher when a small, nervous fellow entered. His daughter, like many Grade 9s who came from small village schools, had not yet adjusted to the town or the high school. She also had some problem with *Of Mice and Men* so I gave her a different book. "We can work it out," I assured the father with a bland smile. He was not assured. "The book is bad," he stammered with both hands clutching his daughter's copy.

"*Of Mice and Men* is good literature and the other students like it a lot," I replied. "I chose it because it's set in a farm area and… well, you've probably met characters like these."

"It curses Our Lord," he said. "It calls him a…a…"

"A what?" I asked.

"Look at page four."

I found a sentence heavily underlined in pencil. "Jesus Christ, you're a crazy bastard."

The father had obviously misread the sentence. "Let me explain," I said. "Jesus Christ is not being called a crazy bastard, Jesus Christ, is used as an expression."

The father looked at me strangely. I was a teacher and I had just sworn in front of him.

Look," I said, seizing my chalk. I wrote out, 'Jesus Christ, you're a crazy bastard.' "The comma separates the expression, 'Jesus Christ', from the rest of the sentence. The speaker says, 'You're a crazy bastard' to his friend, Lennie."

The father rose in horror. I was a teacher and I had just written a blasphemy on the blackboard. He began yelling in a foreign language. He kept yelling as he stomped out and down the hall past 50 or so parents waiting outside various rooms. I did not understand what he said but apparently, everyone else did.

I refused to let it undermine the evening. I stayed calm through the rest of the interviews and parents seemed so impressed by my professional manner that they hardly said a word. It wasn't till the end that I realized what had actually impressed them. As the last parent left, I stood to stretch and I looked behind me at the blackboard. The sentence was still there in large white letters, "Jesus Christ, you're a crazy bastard." They had all seen it. They had probably seen nothing else. The words now seemed directed at me. I was not a master teacher, I was a bumbling fool who would soon be fired. The writing was on the wall.

A week later I was called in by the principal. There were sermons against the book, meetings and numerous phone calls. A highly vocal element wanted the book banned. However, no one had criticized me despite my being an easy target as an outsider, a Jew and a long haired city kid. People stuck to the issues and were surprisingly respectful.

That was not the case in the city. The story hit the media and many people judged the townspeople as a whole, calling them "Bible belters" and "rednecks." Some talked about book banning as if it were a bizarre ritual, like some primitive tribe expelling demons. In fact, I am sure they would have been more respectful of a primitive tribe. I was disappointed that people who knew better gave in to the very prejudices they had imagined in others.

My principal saw both sides but completely supported the book. We attempted to head off the crisis by meeting one of the ministers, a cheerful, articulate man who shook my hand warmly, telling me not to take anything personally. He then told us how shocked he was by a recent radio ad that began, "Gee Whiz! Gee Whiz! Have we got a deal for you!"

Bob Haverluck

I nodded, trying to get his point.

"Don't you see?" he asked. "'Gee Whiz, is a disguised way of saying 'Jesus.' There's blasphemy everywhere!"

I got his point. He would not support us. However, he would give me advice. "Choose books that model good behaviour and that teach moral lessons, books like *Black Beauty*."

"That's fine for children," I said, "but older students need something beyond pure heroes and evil villains, something more realistic."

"One does not outgrow morality," he said.

"*Of Mice and Men* deals with important moral issues," I said. "It just doesn't give a simple answer. We want students to think for themselves."

However, the minister had not read the book. "If you know a book is blasphemous, why read it?" I flashed back to Jerusalem where I had once lived. I heard similar words from an ultra orthodox Jew. He went further. Why read fiction at all? If the Bible and its commentaries have the truth, why trifle with literary fiction? Or with movies or TV? They were breeding grounds for blasphemy.

I didn't understand. I could see that these parents were very protective and wanted to restrict what their children read. But why the focus on blasphemy? *Of Mice and Men* described emotional abuse, violence and murder which seemed far more serious. I disliked swearing but I didn't consider it a crime.

Then I realized that for the fundamentalists among them, profanity was not a crime, it was a deadly sin. My secular education taught me to think freely and to observe the world objectively and without prejudice, even things that frighten or anger me. However, the fundamentalist Jew, Christian or Moslem sees the world in a desperate struggle between good and evil. The sacred must be protected, the profane must be destroyed. I decided it was useless to argue about censorship with people who consider it a crucial defense against the forces of evil.

A week later, there was a knock at my classroom door. The principal, who had fought hard for the book, had lost. He had me gather up all copies from the students. I was not to teach it any further nor discuss why it was removed. I was effectively silenced.

The books were not burned despite the rumours. They were quietly discarded. So was I, though by my own choice. I took a teaching position in Winnipeg where, I decided, I belonged.

Before I left, I witnessed one more sad scene; the school librarian began removing other books that might create a further stir. He hoped to defuse the self-appointed censors who wanted to root through his library for filth. The poor fellow did not realize what a Herculean task he was really embarking on, for once you accept that paranoia you begin to believe what they believe—that sin is everywhere and in every book.

READING AND IMAGINING
A BETTER WORLD

Phyllis Webster

"The imagination. The one reality in this imagined world." [4]

Teaching English can hurt the heart. Each year I teach an astonishing novel called *Imagining Argentina* by Lawrence Thornton. It is set in Argentina during "The Dirty War" from 1976 to 1983 when a junta of generals ran the country after a military coup. Methods of control included snatching people from the street, torturing thousands of people and shutting down any critical media from the press to the theatre. Many people "disappeared," 2000 of whom were drugged and pushed out of airplanes. In total, 9000 people "disappeared." Many of the bodies have never been found. Thornton uses this sorrowful and horrific time as the setting of a novel in which the imagination becomes a real force in the lives of the people in a country which had become a "house full of tears." [5]

The story teaches the history of another land. It helps this teacher to introduce the idea of magic realism and to discuss the poetic imagery which describes both profound beauty and ultimate horror. More importantly, it helps us think beyond our own comfortable lives and for a short while to experience the lives of others which for me, is one of the most important values of studying literature.

• • •

She cowered in the corner protecting her face from the anticipated blows of her jailer. Her screams diminished to soft sobbing as she slowly rolled to the floor and lay still. A profound silence followed. I said very softly, "Thank you. Please pack up your books and leave now."

Jennifer had chosen the role of a "desaparecido," or disappeared, and had enacted what had happened to many young women of the time. Men in green Ford Falcons snatched them from their homes, their schools or the streets. They were raped as part of the torture, and when impregnated were made to carry the foetus to term and to give birth. The generals and their wives then adopted the infants ("children of the night"); the mothers were killed and their bodies buried in unmarked graves.

• • •

Martin Benn, a retired journalist narrates the story of his friend, Carlos, who is a children's playwright and storyteller. Carlos has the ability to "imagine" what has happened to the disappeared and often prophesies their fate. When his wife, Cecelia, and his daughter, Teresa, disappear, he must go on his own journey of despair before one of the women is returned to him.

This year, the class "invited"[6] a general, a driver of a Falcon, a teacher, a professor, a doctor, a lawyer and a priest, some of whom were complicit with the junta while other people turned a blind eye. Some of them, of course, gave up their lives to try to help their fellow beings. Other characters in the novel, the author, the judge who wrote the final report on the Dirty War, and a representative of Amnesty International, also came to the final performance. Another person played the role of Jacob Timerman, a real and very courageous journalist whose paper, *La Opinion*, published stories of government corruption and the oppression of the generals. Timerman was imprisoned, tortured and somehow lived to tell his story and to continue his newspaper. Each student wrote a monologue using the information in the text and other research sources.

The exercise of stepping into the shoes of another human being and imagining why he or she would behave in a certain way is an excellent, if painful, learning experience. I am always astonished that students, who are asked to choose three roles and put them in order of preference, are all very keen to be torturers, the drivers of the Falcons and the generals. All of us need to explore our own desire for "power" and what better way than to do so in our imaginations in the safe environment of the classroom. I always choose a very gentle, tolerant student who often overwhelms us with the power of his or her words. This year, our male torturer left us breathless, speechless and in tears.

· · ·

My name is Pablo Caraballo. I am helping to rid Argentina of its impurities. As I tighten the leather straps around her ankles, I can see her shiver and twitch from fatigue and malnutrition. I stare into her eyes as I listen to the screams and shrieks that flood the cold silence of the concrete walls. I can see her knuckles whiten as she braces herself for the inevitable. She still weeps about her newborn son, who we took from her at birth three days ago. I place the electrodes on the terminals that touch her feet. She wishes that I would shoot her in the back of the neck as I have done for many others who came before her.

I remember when she arrived in the middle of the night, blindfolded and seven months pregnant. She was brought into the basement where she was stripped, numbered, hooded and chained. Several new women came in that night and I remember Roderigo and I walked the halls and decided which prisoners to eliminate to make room. I hated this one in particular because her arrival forced me to stay later than I expected. I missed my son's soccer game as a result. I will take great pleasure as I watch her burn from the inside out.

She is young, maybe only in her early 20s. Her hair is brown, just like my wife's and her eyes are blue like my daughter, Alma's. Alma is my youngest daughter. She was born on a beautiful November day. The sky was a piercing blue. We gave birth at home with all of our family there to welcome a new life into the world. She probably lived in a neighbourhood like the one I live in. But she'll never see her family again. My neighbourhood is a better place without the contamination of our ideals and values brought by disgusting rodents.

Yesterday, Roderigo, the others and I loaded a plane with a hundred prisoners. Their bellies were slit open and their bodies were pushed one by one out of the plane. We watched them slip under the dark surface of the Atlantic to be devoured by sharks. This prisoner was a writer. I will take off a finger each day until her hands are bloodsoaked stumps. She will never write those lies again. If she talks, I'll sever her tongue and feed it to my dogs.

One day, Argentina will return to its former glory...a rich nation, a people united, the Church a part of everyone's life. The Church has brought value to my family's life in a way nothing else could. I dropped my children off at Sunday school this morning before I came to work. Now, I think of them as I finish my job.

I slowly drain the life from her. The volt dial gently turns toward a painful death. Her pupils dilate as her death grip is slowly released. She looks into my eyes and I look into hers. A tear falls from both of our eyes, and I untie the straps.

• • •

A mother of the Plaza da Mayo offers the audience a little respite. She wears a white scarf and carries a sign bearing the name of her loved one who has disappeared. She tells us that she will continue to walk around the Plaza da Mayo every Thursday afternoon with other women who have lost family members until all the disappeared are accounted for. This act of courage during the Dirty War is now a reminder that no government has the right to violate human rights. A judge, who helped write the massive document, *Nunca Mas (Never Again)*, tells us of the abuse during the Dirty War and makes recommendations to prevent future violations.

We end with a visitor from Amnesty International who shows a short clip from an Amnesty International video and tells us how we can help defend people whose rights have been violated. We are challenged to write letters and to join Amnesty International in order to help in the fight against torture, imprisonment and other violations of human rights. This year the representative invited us to learn about the plight of child soldiers, in particular. Several students wrote letters, I am pleased to say.

Yes, teaching English literature hurts my heart. I am frequently reminded that I am human: I belong to a species capable of committing acts of great horror and also of great courage, nobility and kindness. Students understand very well that literature is a necessary part of life…reading not only wounds the heart, it also expands our vision and helps us imagine a better world.

TRANSPORTED

Deborah Schnitzer

I have been waiting quite some time. Many years ago, at the age of 23, with little understanding and with every desire to move beyond the margin of the culture that raised me in a smallish almost northern Ontario town called Sault Ste Marie, I took a job in a very northern Manitoba community called Easterville. I thought the name sounded hopeful. I was young, tending to see only the parts of things.

In truth, I really did not have much of a job. My new husband did. He was going to teach Grades 5 and 6 and 7 and 8. Math. We had emerged from after-degree programs at the University of Calgary with, for him, a degree in Education, and for me, a Master's in English Literature. No money, student loans and this need, I think, in both of us to open something in ourselves, to lean against what loomed as the inevitable settlement in some bedroom community. Mortgaged square feet. Weekend plans. One point five in dependants.

We had no idea where we were going. We rented a tall, spoiled atlas from the University of Calgary library and looked up Easterville. We looked and looked and didn't see anything even though my husband Mendel had a degree in geography. We could not take in Northern Manitoba. We did not take in the fact that the people we were going to "teach" did not speak English as their first language. We had no introduction to cross-cultural anything. A part of a wave of young ones going "west" then perhaps "north," we had little to recommend ourselves except our youth and our ignorance. I had seen fragments of First Nation culture in the Soo, driving past what always remained a nameless reservation at the eastern edge of the city on my way to Toronto, a couple of very silent girls in my Grade 9 French class who lived in a residential Home also at that eastern edge. I never went past the fact that there were "Indians" at the Soo Collegiate Institute where I went to high school and that they didn't talk, only looked back sometimes at the looks we gave them which at best I think were blank.

I remember making eye contact with one of those girls during a French class on, what?—prepositions, verb tenses, articles—I can't remember. We startled ourselves. She seemed to appear at the wrong end of a telescope even though her desk was but one ruler-length away. I just saw her far from me, suspended, drifting in a soundless space. I always see her in this way. The fact that I do means something, some dim consciousness of this non-negotiable space between us which no one ever named but which we felt as disturbingly vacant.

Easterville. I had thought that I would spend this, the second year of our married life, reading all the books I had not had time to read during the crushing process called a Master's. I had loaded up on the Victorians, mostly British, of course, with a couple of 18th century novels, I think, because I believe I was supposed to trace the origin of the genre. These books I had bought at a second hand store—mostly hardcover, beautifully 8 x 8in or smaller and often at 50 cents. But, as circumstances permitted, I became the Principal's relief. I "taught" for half a day, in a Grade 5 classroom. I was supposed to teach Language Arts. Of course, I did not. The children did not know English well enough. I knew no Cree. The workbooks and the readers were opened and opened and opened and we got nowhere very slowly. There were stories about things that barely mattered to me. You can imagine then how they mattered not at all to the children who were supposed to pretend to read them.

Sometimes we sang. I could play seven chords and loved Leonard Cohen, Joan Baez and Joni Mitchell. On Fridays, we moved through the whitefolk songbooks many of us had gone to summer camp with, or worked through rallying songs from the 70-something university campuses we had come from when there was Canadian talk of Viet Nam and Civil Rights—safer talk, quieter protests. Another distance. Another telescope the wrong way round so that what might be the "here" in terms of the struggles of Canadian Aboriginal peoples in this Easterville, for example, was completely uninhabited. Those textbook images of a "vanishing race" never found standing ground outside the pages scripted by writers who romanced a wrong into a seemingly uncontested, inevitable, safer and historical 'long ago.' It was easy to sing protest songs about somewhere else in Easterville.

When I thought I might contribute to this anthology, I knew I could not speak of reading without the groundmaking of my beginnings as a teacher. I was a very bad teacher. I could not connect with the children. They suffered me. And they suffered. Malnutrition, isolation, crumbling infrastructures, alcoholism—the long legacy of government interference and "care." You see these people, the people of Easterville had been transported. I am a Jew. The word transport carries with it special significance, for European highways barely exist for me. I am still startled by the term Autobahn. The civilian traffic mapping that Europe of 1939 to 1945 was built by cattle cars and dead Jews. This persists in me. And the people of Easterville had been the people of Chimawawin, an island in Cedar Lake, an island renowned for its beauty, garden-full, where the people lived off hunting and trapping and fishing, until of course Manitoba Hydro decided to damn the Lake, close that Lake to fishing, "transport" the people to its edge, pour them into government "houses" and a government "school" and, in a series of still-recurring afterthoughts, wonder why the people so spilled, seemed unable to take to the mold prepared for them.

There are not enough words to begin to explain the devastation that ensued. I watched it happen for one year only. I did not manage to read my way through the second-hand novels I had brought to wile away my time in Easterville. My time was useless there. My reading was useless. My education was useless. I had nothing to say. I could not understand what the people said. The tradition of oral telling that lived in them was unknown to me. It was the time when some "white" folks were tramping about in the North trying to translate the legends of Nanabosho into English because someone said that would be good. The people would have their stories in books. Of course, the people might not read those books, nor might they be inclined to transmute their oral culture and tradition into English only, but hey, what could you do? There was nothing much happening in terms of the development of a Cree curriculum, and really, the only way out was THE WAY OUT that spells assimilation. Oh, I could give you that history. But I won't.

Rather, I will tell you why I think reading saves people from themselves and for one another. If I had been able to read anything at all outside of the mold prepared for me by the British and white Canada canon that raised me, I might have understood something about the Canadians in the landscape I was inhabiting. And, if I had been able to read anything outside of the British Canadian version of myself that I had been trained to represent, I might have understood something about the Aboriginal people in the landscape whose lands I had entered as if my own. I don't mean a couple of lines here and there in a magazine, an image or cartoon in a daily newspaper. I mean the sustained immersion in a world whose reality cannot be dismissed or received as residual.

I will tell you that all of "us" in Easterville were reading Herman Wouk's *Winds of War*. I don't know why we cycled together in this way. We all seemed to have come up highway #6 from Winnipeg with a copy of that story, so compelling that I would wake on a Thursday in October, for example, and say, "Hitler invaded Poland" and look for our suitcases, a special photograph, the one wedding gift that we'd brought a thousand miles to this teacherage in Easterville that, yes, had running water when no other house on the reserve did. We were riveted to a story of the world "over there" and did not even begin to see the parallels with this world right here where we made our "living." *Blindness*. A book by José Saramego you have to read because you have to. The refrain—"You gotta read this"—passes from one hand to the other. Because writing stirs people. It takes them and opens them up, helps them live with an idea long enough so that they can see and feel its shape. I am all for being altered, opened.

I did not understand what that meant when we made our way to Easterville because, at that time, and with the little I knew, opened still meant a kind of 60s "think-in," those late and long nights of the soul where we found ourselves. "Opened" after Easterville intensified and expanded the meaning of finding self, for mirrored in me were the very principles and prejudices that had encouraged the colonization of the people whose reality I could not grasp. I was without the stories that held patterns that could at least begin to comprehend the world I had come to. And that's why reading matters. It gives us patterns and those patterns help us see relationships and make connections and comparisons and understand differences and realize the time it takes for a people to tell their story in their terms. You have to sit with that. You can't rush through two lines of poetry or a single short story and find the key words or the "right" answer and repeat them. You have to live with lots of stories and understand carefully how they are made and what you bring to them so that you'll know how you behave in worlds that are not like your own. If you figure that out, you'll figure out what you're capable of, where your sympathies lie, how you make sense of things, what you can imagine, what you cannot, what you do with things that frighten you or mystify, intrigue you. Learning that much requires time and lots of reading diverse, electric and often uncharted worldscapes that take you into and away from that which you think you already know so well.

In 1973, I went to Easterville with the British canon and one or two examples of whiteCanlit. This was important reading. Constricted, but important, for reading some books helps you to read others. But, I had never read Aboriginal literatures. In a very real way, I assumed that the story of the peoples transported to Easterville did not exist in any other terms than the loose anecdotes that circulated among the government employees traveling through. I come from a culture that privileges the written word and I know now more completely how that privileging is questioned within Aborginal cultures, even as there are more and more Aboriginal writers who are working with English and opening its rhythms and patterns so that their stories make the written-down shape they need. I did not know that the story of the people moved to Easterville had much within it that would compare to the story of transported peoples in the *Winds of War*. I do now.

Having read Jeanette Armstrong and Beatrice Culleton Moisonier, and Duncan Mercredi and Beth Brandt and Thomson Highway and Ian Ross and Eden Robinson and Lee Maracle and Basil Johnston and Rita Joe and Maria Campbell and Buffy Sainte-Marie and Annharte and Thomas King and Beth Cuthand and Lenore Keeshig-Tobias and Angela Andrew and Anne Marie Andrew and Caroline Andrew and Mary Adele Andrew and Rose Gregoire and Charlotte Gregoire and Maggie Antuan, and Nympha

Bryne and Carlotte Rich Jordan Wheeler and Daniel David Moses and Marilyn Dumont and Connie Fife and Drew Hayden Taylor and Gregory Scofield and Harry Robinson and Emma Lee Warrior and Ruby Slipperjack and Cecilia Rich and Cecile Rich and Aldea and Augusta Tappage and Maurice Kenny and Joan Crate and Verna Kirkness and John Tetso and Stan McKay and Agnes Grant and Joe McClelland and Alootook Ipellie and Wayne Keon and Emma LaRocque and Bernelda Wheeler and Bill Ballantyne and Mary Young and Darrell Pelletier and Esther Sanderson and Rose Gregoire and Mary Martha Hurley and Natasha Hurley and Pamela Hurley and Gladys Cook and Michael Arvaaluk Kusugak and Joe McLellan and Matrine McLellan and Justine Noah Jack and Madeline Katshinak and Mary Georgette Mistenapeo, and Marie Pokue and Christine Poker and Catherine Poker and Elizabeth Penashue, and Mary Jane Pasteen and Mary Magdeline Nuna, and Mary Jane Nui Roseanna Deerchild and Dave McLeod and and and

I do now.

CLARENCE

Simone Chaput

Clarence, the voice on the phone said his name was Clarence Something or Other... There are so many of them—anonymous for the most part, and almost indistinguishable in their grey winter tatters—I can't be sure I've put the right face to the name. They bend over their soup bowls so that all I can see is the crooked part in their dirty white hair and their stiff-whiskered jaws working the spoon. When we asked him, the voice said, if there was anyone we could call, he dug around in his pocket till he found a piece of paper with your number on it.

I'll come, I said. Even though Paul has rented a good film, and the night is so terribly cold. I'll come. No one should have to die alone.

It's a shared room, 6 hospital beds, people clustered around them like bystanders around a heap of bloodied broken glass. A few televisions have been turned on, the volume low, the pictures spasmodically jumping in the corner of my eye. (At the top of the screen, the words Hot and Not throb with absurdly frantic neon pulse.)

His hair is spread like a gull's wing on the pillow, and in the deep pockets of the leathery face, his milky eyes gleam like opals. I move a little closer, look down, interrupt his gaze. There's a flicker there, a shift in focus, then his eyes are locked on mine. His rough and ropy hands lie still upon the folded hospital sheet, their horn and rawhide as startling in that place as small wild animals, slumbering. I stroke one of them with my winter-cold fingers, let them linger there and warm to his touch. And look, still, into his cloudy eyes and tell him, I'm here, Clarence, and I will stay with you till morning. He does not take his eyes from mine.

It strikes me that this old man and I have never exchanged anything more than a gaze. I recognize him now, saw him many times at Agape

Table, waiting in line for his bread and soup, but cannot remember having heard his voice or seen him smile. He got my number from the billboard in the church hall. And he'd scribbled it on a piece of paper against this very day. On the strength of one look, or two, that had passed between us, he had guessed that I would come, one last time, to feel his eyes upon my face.

I know the worth of words. Know, like St-Ex, that they often get in the way, know, like Camus, the infinite articulateness of a silent gaze. This old Clarence, this broken rack of bone and flesh, looks into my eyes and wordlessly tells me of his fear.

I have no speech prepared to comfort him. I cannot speak to him of what's to come, of the choreography of death, of how one moves from this place to the other. I would like to promise him that there, beyond, on that other shore, there will be no more chilling nights or salty soup. No more of the craven indifference of the world. He will never again sit in a cold, empty room, sharp elbows on sharper knees, hunched over a glowing fag-end and the gnawed bone of his loneliness.

My blood wheels once and stops at the thought of such unspeakable solitude. It is almost beyond imagining. That deep craving for a word, a look, a warm and living touch, forever denied. I think, then, of Bellow's "I want, I want," of his compassion and his heartbreak, I think of his clear insight into the humble yearnings of our mortal flesh: he is the one who reminded us that even Adam, who had God himself to talk to, asked for a human companion…

Clarence has closed his eyes. His breathing is shallow and his skin is slowly turning to wax. My hand still pressed against his, I settle into the chair by his bed and prepare for the long night's watch.

And how shall I pass the hours, I think, in prayer or, like David, by killing time on a knife-edge with the guessing of fragments from poets, or simply in quiet contemplation of the human face before me? There will be night enough, I know, for God, for memory, and for man.

Hold us in your mercy. The words rise up, unbidden, my own eyes are closed, but there is a sudden stirring in the room. Pillows are being plumped up, chair legs are scraping against the floor, good-byes waft through the air, their sad lilt like some old, half-forgotten melody. (On the TV screen, a young girl in a stunningly short skirt flicks her hair for the crowd.) I will soon be left alone, it suddenly occurs to me, with six moribunds and their undisclosed agonies, in the heartless jeering of a studio audience.

I turn away, turn back to him, and watch for stillness to slip beneath his skin. Who is it, I wonder now, who wrote that death is the condition of all natural fulfillment and beauty? And who said that in a world where all is passing, like in a dream, it would be a shame to last forever. We are beautiful, precisely because we are doomed to perish.

I let my eyes follow the lines around Clarence's mouth and eyes, wrinkles as worked and as weather-loved as an old cedar board. His lips are thin, startlingly pale in the deep tan of his face. And I consider the winds that have burnished his cheekbones to a high and fine luster, and the sunshine that sank into his flesh like a wave into the shore. As he watched the river flow beneath the bridges of the city, or sat a moment beneath the spreading branches of the summer elms, did it occur to him that life might only be life when clearly understood as dying? Or did he believe, like Da Vinci, that he was learning how to live when, in fact, he was learning how to die?

His eyes move beneath the heavy lids. In what dreams, I wonder, among what dull roots of memory and desire. And I consider what other man might have been assassinated in the one that lies so still before me. An artist, perhaps, a lover, the tender keeper of an unrequited flame. Or a great tall man, with the voice of drums and the heart of a child, and the gall of a thousand, and the strength of conviction. But it hardly matters now. In the death of this one old man, this paltry thing, this tattered coat upon a stick, is gathered all life, all death. And I know that as I mourn his passing, it is for myself that I grieve.

I cannot take my eyes from his face and its slow transfiguration. No longer unknown, no longer indistinguishable; it is my own. Though made of clay and spit, though seamed with imperfection, it bears upon it the trace of God's hand. I lift my fingers to brush the stark white hairs from his forehead and am stricken by the fragility of the bone there, by the uncertain heartbeat in the hollow of the temple. And I think: temple, indeed. (From the TV screen, I hear a voice say, "I give you 7.5 for your face, 8.2 for your body, 8.6 for your sex appeal.")

This vigil, I know now, will pass like a dream. And I become aware all at once of a feeling taking root in my heart. It is gratitude, stirring like the green blades of spring in dark winter earth: I am grateful to this silent old man for having entrusted his dying to me. And as I watch with him, and wait with him, I know that the grace that gathers in this moment is bigger than him, and bigger than me. We are the world, Clarence and I, and our silent communion is filled with the voices of men and angels, singing him to his rest.

With the generous (if passive) collaboration of Antoine de St-Exupéry, Albert Camus, Saul Bellow, Earle Birney, Marguerite Yourcenar, Leonardo da Vinci, T.S. Eliot, Margaret Laurence, W.B. Yeats and Shakespeare.

NAVIGATING THE WORDS

Catherine Hunter and Karen Zoppa

Hi there Karen,

As we discussed, I'm thinking about the value of literature in one's education and in one's life. It seems to me that there are two broad ways in which to approach the topic. On one hand, you could argue that there are plenty of practical benefits (social, financial, etc.). On the other hand, one could go for a good old philosophical argument, assuming that art has intrinsic value. I'm much more tempted by the latter, but feel I must make some nod toward the former as well.

Don't feel you need to respond to this as there is nothing much here yet to respond to! Just wanted to say I am thinking about this project and will send some meditations soon.

xxx
Catherine

Dear Catherine:

I'm thinking about the struggle involved in getting my students to actually read a whole book and discuss it in class. I'm wondering whether they would buy the intrinsic value argument or if it's just another mark generator for their "careers."

I want to approach this project concretely, through the conversation we have been having for many years about our life in the classroom with our students. As usual, I have begun our October term with a study of *Heart of Darkness*. My intention is always multifaceted. I want them first of all to experience reading a dense, complex and evocative text. I think this text is an excellent candidate for its brevity and for its narrative and philosophical depth. I want them to experience reading on at least two levels of meaning: here, the easiest are the surface elements of the story and the psychological symbolism. I want them to hear "voice" through the example of Marlow. I want to them to learn how to explicate a quotation in relation to the whole—to analyze, synthesize, and evaluate. I want them to "see" the "truth" that Conrad offers. I am nuts.

As usual, as we begin and I ask them some simple comprehension questions, I am met with a whine cellar: "this book is too hard," "I don't like it—it's boring," "this sucks." After I suggest that boredom is usually a function of a boring personality, they admit that they don't like the long multiclause sentences or the vast vocabulary. "It's so confusing." I sigh and again abandon the fantasy that maybe they have actually read the book. So I have to set them up.

I do. I draw them a map of Marlow's journey; a map of the plot structure; and then a brief bio of Conrad. I ask them to picture Marlow with a pipe and flask of rum and a rumble in his voice. I read the opening sequence to them, doing my best impersonation of a sailor. They listen. They respond to questions about atmosphere and foreshadowing.

This is painful. I want to quit.

Later,

Karen

Hi Karen,

I'm interested in your description of Conrad's text as "dense, complex, and evocative." I think you're putting your finger on something important here. Why read *Heart of Darkness,* as opposed to, say, a *National Geographic* article about the Congo River or a political essay about colonialism? The answer is partly because Conrad's novel is dense and complex and evocative.

Those long, multi-clause sentences, cause of so much complaint, create the density. What is the point of wading through such density? they ask. Why not simply say what you mean and mean what you say? I think the point in wading through density is that it is the only way to learn what language is and how it works.

For example, I always enjoy teaching Dylan Thomas's "A Refusal to Mourn the Death, by Fire, of a Child in London." Here is the first sentence, guaranteed to make students groan and/or weep:

Never until the mankind making
Bird beast and flower
Fathering and all humbling darkness
Tells with silence the last light breaking
And the still hour
Is come of the sea tumbling in harness

And I must enter again the round
Zion of the water bead
And the synagogue of the ear of corn
Shall I let pray the shadow of a sound
Or sow my salt seed
In the least valley of sackcloth to mourn

The majesty and burning of the child's death.

Well, the first thing I'd say is that if you can parse that sentence you understand sentence structure. And usually that's the first thing I do when I teach this poem. I ask, "where is the grammatical subject of the sentence?" Sometimes it takes a while for the students to figure out that the subject is "I" and the predicate verb is "shall never let pray or sow." But they always do! Studying this dense language, wending their way through the tangled jungle of it, they find their way. (Or at least, the ones who know a little grammar do. Some of them think that the subject of the sentence is "Never." I explain that the subject must be a noun or pronoun. "Oh," they say, "is it *making*?")

Thomas's language, like Conrad's, is highly complex—especially in this particular poem. But I believe that complex thought requires complex language, and also that one cannot understand complex language without engaging in complex thought. Thus, the poem exercises the mind.

Sometimes when putting forth their interpretations, my students will say, "Well, I think what the poet is trying to say is…" Their phrasing is very revealing, implying as it does that the poor poet is handicapped in some way, incapable of clear speech and struggling in his or her muddled way to express some simple idea. Who taught them that density and complexity were aspects of language to be gotten through or gotten past? They seem to want to boil everything down to some simplistic essential. "This poem's about death," they'll say; "that one's about love." They are ready and willing to "decode" each poem, to get to its "real" meaning, as quickly as possible please, and turn the page. They ignore the language, as if the poem were made out of some other kind of stuff (mud? snow? macaroni?). Who taught them to read like this?

We could simply paraphrase Thomas's sentence: "I will never mourn this child." But if that's all he wanted to say, he could have, and would have, simply said it like that. We don't go through the trouble of untangling the syntax simply to retrieve that one bare naked idea. Thomas's first sentence expresses several beautiful and complicated ideas, and there is no other way to express them.

But I suppose that, in a culture that can't be bothered to put the "Q" in "Kwik Mart," our students have rarely been exposed to the notion that language is important, that it might mean something.

More later,
Catherine

Hello sweet muse:

Quite (or should that be kwite) a mouthful. Your question is disturbing and stimulating: what is the point of wading through such density?

My first thought is, because the content demands it. What content? asks the curriculum designer at the Department of Education. The Language Arts classroom is not for teaching content—content is merely an instrument for teaching language, right?

Hold me back. On second thought, let me go: The content of Conrad's novella, or Thomas's poem, demands complexity. The particular experience these poets (if I may use that term broadly) want to communicate requires certain rhythms in syntax, atypical, even arresting vocabulary, and especially time. The reader's experience of navigating a lengthy, multi-clause descriptive sentence is like traveling into a tunnel or an alley of trees or up a river coiled with bends that obscure the next vista: it is exhausting and exhilarating, at first, but later it can be seen whole, from a distance, revealing the particularity of its shape and aim.

For example, although I always bitch when we begin to study *Heart of Darkness*, by Part Two, the students become more willing travellers, and begin to hear Marlow's voice, his humour and cynicism. By the time we come to his summary statement in Part Three, they are able to hear the content in relation to his journey and their own experience. They hear him say "Destiny! My destiny! Droll thing life is, that mysterious arrangement of merciless logic for futile purpose. The most you can hope from it is some knowledge of yourself, that comes too late…" and they understand the unpredictability of life, the relentless character of necessity, the inevitable fate which meets us all while still seeing that what redeems all of this is the determination to be honest with ourselves. Or at least they understand that this is Conrad's character's lesson—and they can take it or leave it. This sentence is discussed for about three minutes—some of them understand how to approach adjective phrases by this time—and they are more interested in stating what they gather Marlow has "learned." Of course, in order to hear what Marlow is saying, they had to hear him share "the particular blackness of that experience." The sentence serves that experience, not vice versa.

So, I say to the imaginary bureaucrat, the content of the texts I teach is primary, because if language doesn't serve communication, then what the hell is it for? and besides, o worshipper of discrete rhetorical skills (said bureaucrat), my students are able to read densely and complexly now, so they have more than a chance to communicate richly themselves.

I want to end this part of our conversation by saying that I do not mean to discount the beauty, power and enjoyment of language—its sounds, shapes, textures and arrangements—in and of themselves. But I will argue that this is a secondary quality.

Karen

Dear Karen,

I'm interested by the fact that we seem to be approaching this topic on two different fronts. It appears that I'm talking about language, while you are talking about content. I'm saying language is ignored in the classroom, while you're saying content is ignored. Yet we're both in agreement. I think this is because, *in literature*, language and content are not separate, nor were they ever separate, despite the best-laid plans of mice and curriculum designers. And perhaps it is this very aspect of literature that makes it so necessary, and so irreplaceable, in the classroom.

The study of literature differs qualitatively from the study of other "texts," such as editorials or advertisements. In literature, content is not merely an instrument for teaching language, nor is language merely a conduit for content. And it is only literature that allows us to see this fully. Conrad's moral and aesthetic vision can't be swept aside for a quick grammar lesson; Dylan Thomas's convoluted syntax can't be straightened out, like a tangled garden hose, so that the information can flow more freely.

Dylan Thomas's dense language doesn't prevent us from reading the poem; it *is* the poem. And when the students engage with his language, they can read the poem quite clearly. Thomas's first sentence is full of rich, allusive imagery that conjures all kinds of associations in the attentive reader's mind. In the classroom, we ask a lot of questions as we read. We can see the last light breaking and the sea tumbling in harness, before we understand what they mean. Then we ask, well, when does the last light break? When does the sea stand still? Never? At the end of time? In any case, it's the time when the poet must "enter again the round/Zion of the water bead." What does that mean? (Usually at this point, someone mentions death again.) We try to picture the "Zion of the water bead." We might not understand it right away, but then, when we come to that image of the "synagogue of the ear of corn," we realize that both images have something to do with the merging of the spiritual and the natural world. And wait a minute, isn't a "synagogue" a place where Jews worship, and didn't Thomas write this poem during the holocaust? And we're off… Oh my goodness, we're *thinking!*

There is no other way that Thomas could have raised these particular ideas, and no other way that Conrad could have raised his ideas, except by using exactly the language they used. Literature is an art form that uses language as its medium. One can no more understand a poem by ignoring its language than one could understand a still-life painting by eating a bowl of fruit. The language and the content are inextricable in literature and, lo, here I am back at my initial quandary. Shall I say that there is a practical benefit to the study of literature? Or shall I say that the experience has intrinsic value?

There is of course a practical benefit to the experience of reading *Heart of Darkness* or "A Refusal to Mourn." We increase our vocabulary, expand our imaginations, exchange ideas, practice our grammar, exercise our powers of reasoning, and learn a little bit about the ivory trade or the Second World War. We hone our interpretive skills—what did the writer "mean," exactly? Conrad's intent has been the subject of debate for over a hundred years, now, and when we enter that debate we see that language is slippery, that meaning can be constructed selectively to suit the interpreter's interests, *that meaning is constructed.* If we're paying attention, we also learn ways to express ourselves more powerfully and persuasively. There is also a deep, moral dimension to these works, and surely morality—no matter what else it might be—is a practical issue as well. Conrad and Thomas raise serious ethical questions, daring us to ask ourselves why we are here on this planet, what responsibilities we might have toward others, what debts we might owe for the lives we are living and why we should care. These works elicit our empathy, stretch our emotional intelligence, encourage us to consider the points of view of those other than ourselves.

But aside from the practical benefits, we also develop the aesthetic dimensions of ourselves, a facet of the human animal that has been sorely neglected in this culture. The aesthetic dimension of the human being, I would argue, should be developed along with his or her physical, emotional, spiritual and intellectual dimensions. This can only be accomplished through the study of art. It cannot be accomplished through the reading of newspapers, magazine articles, campaign speeches, political cartoons or whatever else passes for a "text" these days. When your students travel through Conrad's jungle down the long, winding rivers of his sentences, they're not just learning syntax. They begin by engaging in detail with the individual nouns and verbs and adjectival clauses, but eventually the book itself, to use your words, "can be seen whole, from a distance, revealing the particularity of its shape and aim." The carefully crafted structure of Conrad's work is composed of those sentences, and it's only after we have read them that we can see the artist's design, which is but a glimpse of his larger vision.

One might argue that there is no practical value to art. But then again, one might argue that there is no artistic value to practicality. It is all very well to "go out and get a job," but once you've got that job, once you've paid the rent and bought the groceries, what are you going to do then?

Good night,
Catherine

Dear Catherine:

Thank you for the last bit—I say YES to all of the above. If I may have a last word, I'll just offer an observation that confirms these insights for me. We are reading *King Lear* together in my English Literary Focus class right now. I do this to support them and to give them the opportunity to see that they do understand Shakespeare's rather taut cadences in this play. What never ceases to amaze and move and teach *me* is the way they *care* for these poetic constructions, these Lears and Cordelias and Fools constituted by naught but words. My spirit rose particularly today when their young glossy eyes "told with silence" the power of three little words to destroy a king: "What need one?" sneers Goneril as she grinds the remnants of Lear's dignity and identity into the dust. I know their spirits will rise at Cordelia's impossibly succinct expression of unconditional love: "No cause." This is far from the serpentine density of Conrad or Thomas, and yet these short phrases open into vast pools of meaning for these readers, these imaginers through the word, and again affirms that the word is the living thing. Amen.

Karen xx

READ THIS!

"I WAS LIKE WOW!" ON THE VALUE OF STUDYING LITERATURE IN THE LANGUAGE ARTS CLASSROOM

Valdine Clemens

Literature: n. *written works, especially those regarded as having artistic merit. *books and writings on a particular subject. *leaflets and other material used in advertising or to give advice.
—*Concise Oxford English Dictionary,* 10th ed.

In *The Time Machine* (1895), H. G. Wells explores the possibility that at the end of the nineteenth century, humanity may have reached its apex, as far as its achievements in culture and civilization are concerned. His late-Victorian "Time Traveller" moves 802,701 years into the future. The Time Traveller, having imbibed some of the socialist and utopian ideas of his day, assumes that the "whole world will be intelligent, educated, and co-operating" (48). His first impressions seem to confirm this assumption of inevitable improvement: "The air was free from gnats, the earth from weeds or fungi; everywhere were fruits and sweet and delightful flowers; brilliant butterflies flew hither and thither. The ideal of preventive medicine was attained. Diseases had been stamped out. I saw no evidence of any contagious diseases during all my stay" (48).

The Time Traveller goes on to observe that in this new world there appears to be no toil, no sign of social or economic struggle or inequality, no commerce. A tranquil and seemingly perfect world—except that when he tries to learn the language of the Eloi, the first group of humanity's descendants that he meets, he feels "like a schoolmaster amidst children." He persists, however, and soon has "a score of noun substantives at least to my command." Then he gets "to demonstrative pronouns, and even the verb 'to eat'" (45). As he soon discovers, the Eloi neither read nor write.

Some readers today, including teachers of high school LA in Manitoba and elsewhere, might have difficulty figuring out exactly what Wells is getting at here. The teaching of English grammar as a distinct component of LA has not been offered In Manitoba schools for decades. When was that momentous decision made, and by whom? And why is it considered essential to study the grammar of other languages, yet not of English? Nouns? Verbs? Demonstrative pronouns?

The Time Traveller goes on to observe that the Eloi show a lack of interest in abstract subjects and become easily fatigued by mental effort (45), and his earlier observations help to explain this situation for anyone with a grasp of basic grammar. The Eloi's language has become utterly unimaginative, unvaried and utilitarian. Their vocabulary is extremely limited. (Did George Orwell read *The Time Machine*? My guess is yes.)

Notions of "social darwinism"—the inevitability of survival of the fittest in the social sphere—permeate Wells's novella. The fate of the lazy Eloi is to be eaten by the cannibalistic Morlocks, and the more industrious Morlocks, with their "mechanical intelligence," have the upper hand, despite the fact that they live below ground. Yet these two seemingly antithetical groups suffer from the same deficiency. Both are illiterate and inarticulate.

One consequence of this loss of "culture," in Wells's story, is moral degeneration, demonstrated in part by the Eloi's indifference to the welfare of their fellows (one of the Eloi would have drowned in a stream while the others watched, had the Time Traveller's intervention not saved her). "Moral degeneration" is a phrase with particular Victorian connotations, but it's one that remains, I would say, quite relevant to today's fledgling democratic societies (whether 200+ years old or just emerging) and to the larger global economy that is both enabling and threatening the democratic impulse.

Wherever the study of language and literature occurs, it has the potential to enhance students' awareness of both their own and others' worlds. Literature provides opportunities for thinking and talking about society, ethics, the meaning and significance of experience and the larger questions of human existence.[7] Most students in the Middle and Senior levels have reached the age of judgement: a time when such issues often feel

READ THIS!

especially pressing. The opportunity to engage in literature—and in any discussion of it that explores the ethical implications of a situation, or the psychological motivation of a character, or the varieties of cultural difference, or the ways that a certain story or poem can stir a reader with the simple intensity of its eloquence, beauty and 'truth'—can be invaluable.

Basic literacy itself has the power to enhance precision in expression and understanding. A recent CBC program (FM: January 31, 2002) reported that in some northern Canadian communities the increasing literacy of the Cree youth, who have been learning a written code that augments the oral transmission of their linguistic heritage, has had the effect of developing a "more highly nuanced" use of their native language.

This is where the question of defining "literature" comes in. What a vague phrase for the *OED* to use: "artistic merit"—one that, for some, calls up notions of elitism, rejection of diversity and innovation, restrictive "canonization" imposed by the privileged and powerful. But the distinction between the *OED*'s first and third definitions should not be underestimated. "Leaflets and other material used in advertising or to give advice" are a very different matter from works of "artistic merit," however slippery that last term may be.

Most students already know that language is a form of power, both positive and negative, expansive and restrictive. Learning terms for the varieties of "media massage" that surround them every day—euphemism, jargon, hyperbole, slogans, propaganda, overt/covert messages—can only empower students. They want and need to examine these questions: Who or what determines usage? How do the conventions of a given language change? How do social values affect language usage, and vice versa?

A useful exercise might be to examine the excessive jargon, obfuscation, and general mangling of the English language in our current LA Curriculum Guide—though I suppose that any teacher who tried to do so might run the risk of being fired. (Was no-one on the committee aware that they were using the word "outcomes" euphemistically—implying that the *goals, aims, objectives* of the curriculum have already been realized?)

When *The Time Machine* first appeared, public education was becoming more widely accessible to "the masses," and the electronic age was just beginning. The concerns he raised in this novel seem all the more pressing a century later in the Information Age, when the high-speed communication made possible by electronic media makes the literacy of the world's future citizens an even more urgent issue.

Speaking locally, I would like to suggest a few areas that in my opinion need more emphasis in the Manitoba LA classroom today. The development of clarity and precision in writing skills is essential.[8] Students should become familiar with the tools used to establish or discern meaning, such as dictionaries and thesauri. There should be discussion of such issues as slang, "American" and "Canadian" spelling, connotation and denotation, and so forth. Students need to be exposed to a *variety* of written materials that will help them develop a larger and more precise vocabulary. Vocabulary-building games and exercises can actually be fun.

Students also need to be engaged in the issue of sentence structure—the idea that sentences are structures with identifiable parts that generally fit together in certain ways. The idea that all communication involves a *shared code.* Why a poorly constructed sentence may not make sense to anyone else, or even to the writer a few days later. What a sentence fragment is… Again, students need to be exposed to a wide range of written materials that will help them understand and appreciate the varieties and complexities of sentence structure. They also need to learn about punctuation and why it matters. (Recently, in a first-year English literature class where we were discussing the use of punctuation in poetry, an embarrassed-looking student came up to me, pointed to an exclamation mark and asked what it was called.)

It's important as well that students learn to appreciate the fact that "shared" codes differ, and that different codes can reflect very different perceptual and belief systems (what is "time"? what is "guilt"?) One way to examine the implications of such differences is to read two or more different translations of the same text; another is to encourage monolingual students to learn at least one language other than English.

Many LA teachers appreciate the fact that helping students to develop strong reading comprehension skills includes teaching them strategies such as note-taking, highlighting, and, above all, in longer works of literature, pattern recognition. What is a *motif*? What is a *plot*? What is *irony*? What is *satire*? It is also essential that the whole class reads *together in detail* some of the same texts—novels, poems, plays, essays, newspaper articles—and that students are given the opportunity to assess their own comprehension of the information by comparing and contrasting their own readings with those of other students. The information may be as basic as factual detail, or as subtle as psychological insight or poetic/symbolic resonance. I include this seemingly common-sense advice partly because my own son had a teacher who declared that students' "freedom to choose" their own texts was "essential in the Language Arts classroom"—a statement which struck me as a cover-up for the teacher's desire for freedom from the task of offering any guidance to the students. (Also, of course, there's no reason why the students themselves can't recommend texts to study together.)

Discussion and debate can also help students both to appreciate the ways that a work of literature may give rise to a variety of legitimate interpretations, and to learn how personal bias and experience can affect, enhance, or, yes, even detract from one's response to a particular text.

One important area that does receive stress in the current LA Curriculum Guide is the aim of encouraging creativity in writing and reading. I would just like to emphasize that this goal is entirely congruent with the two already discussed. For example, "playing around" with words and forms such as puns, neologisms, metaphors, similes, limericks, and all sorts of poetry helps to enlarge vocabulary. Playing around with a given text by substituting nouns for other nouns, verbs for other verbs, and so forth, helps to develop awareness of grammar. Playing Scrabble helps to develop spelling skills. Individual and collaborative writing projects in which students are asked to study and then employ a variety of forms (memoir, poem, song, play, story) help to develop a greater understanding of genre and craft. Undertaking a revision process develops precision in expression and also teaches the old adage that creativity can at times be 10% inspiration, 90% perspiration. Performing drama can make the literature come alive. Assessing a novel (or story)—to-film transition can make students more aware of the differences between visual and verbal messages, as can inter-art responses to the literature.

Finally, one goal of LA education that does not, in my opinion, receive adequate stress in the current Curriculum Guide is the development of the capacity for sustained critical thinking. There are two main ways in which students can develop this capacity. One is by *reading extended literature* such as novels, plays, essays, histories, and so forth. The other is by *writing essays.* In the last few years of their secondary education, students need to learn about the following elements of essay writing: thesis statement, topic sentence, paragraph organization, logic.

The issue of teacher's accreditation is a pertinent one here. The above activities can be handled effectively only by teachers who themselves are reasonably fluent in language arts: teachers who read and are passionate about reading, teachers who understand the basics of English grammar and have strong vocabularies. There are many such talented and dedicated teachers today in the LA classrooms of Manitoba. Unfortunately, the current system allows any teacher, regardless of her or his educational background, the freedom to teach at any level, even though, as most people recognize, students' capacities and needs change significantly from the elementary to the secondary years. *This flaw in the system is a serious one that needs to be addressed.* And it can be addressed only by a political leadership that is ready and willing to challenge the sludge-like influence of the bureaucracies, both governmental and unionized, that have the power to choke the life out of LA education.

Many parents today already appreciate the pragmatic value of language fluency for individual success in a competitive market economy—whether or not they accept the egalitarian impulse that is expressed so often in what is called *literature,* in works like *The Time Machine.* I would suggest to all parents, especially those who are also concerned about the essential role of education in maintaining a civil society, that you need to speak out. Have a look at the current curriculum guide. Pay close attention to what's happening in your children's Language Arts classrooms. Contact your children's teachers, and, if you still have concerns, contact the principal. And, if you still have concerns, contact your trustees, your MLAs, your Minister of Education. Contact us!

CONTRIBUTORS

DAVID BERGEN's first novel, *A Year of Lesser*, won the 1996 Manitoba Book of the Year Award and was a Book-of-the-Month Club selection. Bergen was awarded the 2000 CBC Literary Prize for Fiction and his story, "Life Before Nietzsche," was selected for the *Toronto Life* magazine 2000 Summer Fiction issue. *See the Child*, his second novel, has been published in France and the U.S. *The Case of Lena S.*, his latest novel, was shortlisted for the Governor General's Award and won the Carol Shields Winnipeg Book Award.

NEIL BESNER is Dean of Humanities at the University of Winnipeg. He writes mainly on Canadian literature; his most recent books are an edited collection of work on Carol Shields (2003) and a translation into English of a Brazilian biography of the poet Elizabeth Bishop (2002).

MELANIE CAMERON was born in Kitchener-Waterloo in 1971. Her book, *Holding the Dark* (1999, The Muses' Company), was shortlisted for the Eileen MacTavish Sykes Award for Best First Book by a Manitoba Writer. Melanie was also shortlisted for the John Hirsch Award for Most Promising Manitoba Writer in both 1999 and 2001. Her second book of poetry, *wake*, was published by The Muses' Company in the fall of 2003. Melanie is Poetry Co-Editor of *Prairie Fire* magazine, and is currently completing her third book.

DI BRANDT is an award winning poet who presently teaches English literature and creative writing at the University of Windsor.

RHIAN BRYNJOLSON is the author of *Art and Illustration for the Classroom*. Her illustrations appear in books by Peter Eyvindson and Joe McLellan, and on *Sesame Street*. Rhian taught at the Winnipeg Art Gallery, toured with Manitoba Arts Council programs, and now teaches in an inner city school.

SIMONE CHAPUT is a teacher of language and literature and the author of three novels and a book of short stories. She lives in Winnipeg with her husband and their two daughters.

VALDINE CLEMENS teaches English literature at the University of Winnipeg and has a son in public school. She joined MACRO after learning that some teachers and school administrators see the new curriculum guide as sanctioning a no-content approach to language arts education.

JOSHUA J.M. GRUMMETT is a Grade 11 AP student at John Taylor Collegiate with five main facets to his life: performing, ranting, thinking, escaping (through games and speculative fiction) and writing. He plans to become a journalist at some point. Later on, maybe. After he turns eighteen.

BOB HAVERLUCK is artist-in-residence in the Faculty of Theology at the University of Winnipeg. His work has appeared in *Harpers, New Statesman, This Magazine* and *Border Crossings.* He has written and illustrated two books on peacemaking: *Love Your Enemies and Other Neighbours* and *Peace: Peace/Conflict.*

JAN HORNER attended Lincoln School and Westwood Collegiate in Winnipeg, and has fond memories of English classes with Mrs. Young and Mr. Finnbogasin. She has published two books of poetry with Turnstone Press and was the winner of the first McNally Robinson Book of the Year Prize for *Recent Mistakes* (1988).

CATHERINE HUNTER's books include the poetry collection *Latent Heat,* the mystery thriller *The Dead of Midnight,* and, most recently, the novella *In the First Early Days of My Death.* She teaches English and Creative Writing at the University of Winnipeg.

PAMELA LOCKMAN has loved books since she started going to the public library with her dad when she was about three. She has taught for a long time, starting in her parents' garage when she was about seven. There is no end in sight for her enjoyment of literature or teaching!

SHELDON OBERMAN is a storyteller and award winning author of 12 books for adults and children including *The Always Prayer Shawl, The Wisdom Bird* and *The Shaman's Nephew: A Life in the Far North.* He travels widely, storytelling and teaching the art of personal, fictional and traditional stories. www.sheldonoberman.com

READ THIS!

A proud U of W graduate of the B.Ed program (1981), **MARG ROSE** has 20 years experience teaching senior high, college and adult education learners. She now serves as Exec. Director of Literacy Partners of Manitoba, while pursuing her M. Ad. Ed. Living and loving language is her raison d'etre!

Essayist and novelist, **JOHN RALSTON SAUL**'s latest book is *On Equilibrum*, published by Penguin Canada.

Part of MACRO since its beginnings and an English teacher at the University of Winnipeg, **DEBORAH SCHNITZER** appreciates being part of this collection and working with those who felt its possibility. She is certain that reading books helps us dream, connect, aspire and act creatively, carefully and responsibly. Two recent book projects include *The Madwoman in the Academy: 43 Women Boldly Take on the Ivory Tower*, co-edited with Deborah Keahey, and *Story After Story: Canadians Bend Bound Theology*.

SHARON SELBY is a Canadian writer and teacher.

PHYLLIS WEBSTER teaches English and Journalism at The Collegiate at The University of Winnipeg. Michael Fishbach, the writer of the torturer's monologue, is one of many wonderful students to whom she has had the pleasure of introducing works of literature. When not reading, Phyllis enjoys riding her 1937 CCM bicycle around Wildwood Park with her little rabbit, Nudge, in the basket.

DAVID WELHAM has been in (and out of) teaching and writing since 1976; currently he works at the Collegiate at the University of Winnipeg where he struggles to learn how to teach Creative Writing. At home he is a dad who listens to his daughter's advice: "Don't sing and don't dance."

KAREN ZOPPA teaches English, Philosophy and Religious Studies at the University of Winnipeg Collegiate when she isn't writing or chairing MACRO. She has been Chair of MACRO since 1999.

NOTES

1. E. Long, & S. Middleton, *Patterns of Participation in Canadian Literacy and Upgrading Programs.* (Toronto: ABC Canada, 2001).

2. Organization for Economic and Cooperative Development. *Literacy, Economy and Society: Results of the International Adult Literacy Survey.* (Paris: Statistics Canada, OECDn, 1996).

3. L. Pearson, Address on the Launch of the International Forum on Canadian Children's Literature: "The Fun of Reading," *National Library of Canada Bulletin,* 34,5: (April 2, 2002): 19-20.

4. Ibid., 21-22.

5. Lawrence, Thornton, *Imagining Argentina.* (Toronto: Bantam Books, 1988), p. 79. Thank you to Michael Fishbach for the use of his monologue.

6. The word "invited" for this exercise means that each student chooses a role from the novel and prepares a monologue of about 800 words. We gather in a quiet room lit by candles. Each student walks quietly to the front and reads her own work. We do not clap or speak at any point. When everyone has read, it is important to return to our own world by speaking our names and saying who we are.

7. Some of these comments have been paraphrased from a letter sent to MACRO by Manitoba's former Minister of Education, Drew Caldwell.

8. Some of this material has been adapted from the *Guide to First-Year English Literature and Language Study at the University of Winnipeg.*

ACKNOWLEDGEMENTS

An earlier version of "In Defence of Public Education" by John Ralston Saul was published in *Horizons* (the official publication of the Canadian Teachers' Federation) in Fall 2002.

The illustration by Rhian Brynjolson in her piece "Why Do We Need Books?" (page 65) was originally published in her book *Foster Baby* (Pemmican Publications: Winnipeg, 1996).

Sheldon Oberman's "Censorship Issue—Of Mice and Men" was originally published in the "Slice of Life" column in the *Winnipeg Free Press* (Feb 23, 2000).